DEAR BRITTA
a memoir

PHILLIP KUCHMAN

Copyright © 2020 Phillip Kuchman

All rights reserved. No part of this publication may be reproduced or transmitted in any form or by any means, electronic or mechanical, including photocopy, recording, or any information storage and retrieval system, without prior written permission from the copyright holder.

ISBN-13: 9798646960093

Dear Britta is a work of memoir. It reflects the author's present recollections of experiences over time. Some names and identifying details have been changed to protect the privacy of individuals.

Unless otherwise indicated, Scripture quotations are from the *New World Translation of the Holy Scriptures*, 1984 or 2013 editions, published by the Watchtower Bible and Tract Society of New York, Inc.

Quotations may have formatting added for artistic effect. Any formatting present in the original text is noted as such.

All quotations remain the intellectual property of their respective copyright holders. All copyrighted material has been used per the "fair use" provisions of copyright law.

All trademarks are the property of their respective owners. The author is not associated with any product or vendor mentioned in this book.

DEAR BRITTA

Contents

Glossary	viii
Prologue	1
Truth	8
Bethel	19
Entertainment	39
College	71
Watchtower, Inc.	91
Work	127
Sex	155
Growth	180
Law	242
Intuition	286
Death	291
Life	304
Helpful Resources	371
References	377

"Tell them to work at good, to be rich in fine works... so that they may get a firm hold on the real life."
— 1 Timothy 6:18, 19

"Is this the real life? Is this just fantasy?"
— "Bohemian Rhapsody," Queen

Glossary

Annual Meeting—an annual one-day conference held at JW world headquarters. A few thousand Witnesses are selected to attend. Used in recent years to announce new developments in the Organization or doctrine.

Anointed—JWs believe that in the two thousand years since Jesus' death, 144,000 spirit-anointed men and women have been chosen to go to heaven upon their death. They will all rule with Jesus as kings (there are no queens in JW cosmology) and priests over the earth. All other JWs have the hope of living forever in a paradise on earth. Currently, around twenty thousand JWs (out of around eight million total) say they are anointed, including all Governing Body members. (There are no women in JW heaven. I'm not sure Sister Whelpton, the wizened ninety-something anointed woman I knew as a child, had quite considered the transgender implications of this particular JW teaching.)

Assembly—one- or two-day conference of about one thousand JWs, held once or twice a year

Apostate—a JW who leaves for doctrinal reasons. Often preceded by Disassociation. Considered very dangerous by the Organization. Should be shunned by current members.

Attendant—a Brother at an Assembly or Convention assigned to direct traffic, maintain order, and take attendance

Awake—the second main magazine JWs print, a companion to the *Watchtower* magazine. Often focuses more on science and current events in comparison to the *Watchtower*'s religious focus.

Baptism—whole-body immersion in a pool to signify full membership as a JW. Baptisms are done at Assemblies or Conventions. Preceded by first becoming an Unbaptized Publisher. Baptismal candidates must be approved by local Elders. This is done by considering their conduct as well as two hours of open-book oral exams on JW teachings.

Bethel—a Hebrew word meaning "House of God," the name given to all JW branch offices that oversee each country; also, the name for the world headquarters facilities in the United States. Staffed by Bethelites who volunteer in exchange for room and board.

Bethelite—a JW who lives and works full time at Bethel

Bible Student—what Jehovah's Witnesses were called prior to 1931. Also, a potential convert with whom a JW is meeting on a weekly basis for indoctrination in JW teachings. A JW textbook and a Bible are used. The session is called a "Bible study." The goal is for the student to begin attending meetings at the Kingdom Hall, become an Unbaptized Publisher, and subsequently get baptized as one of Jehovah's Witnesses.

Brother—the title by which JWs refer to other male Witnesses: "Brother Jones," "Sister Smith." From Matthew 23:8, "[A]ll of you are brothers."

Car group—a group of JWs preaching. At each congregation's daily morning meeting for Field Service, the Brother conducting the meeting spends a few minutes on a Bible topic, and then arranges everyone in groups of generally four people per car. Since it is usually first asked if anyone has already made arrangements to work with someone, a Sister—who otherwise would have no power to direct matters—can set up a car group beforehand, and exercise a small bit of autonomy.

Circuit—group of approximately twenty Congregations in proximity to each other; each circuit is managed by a Circuit Overseer

Circuit Assembly—see Assembly.

Circuit Overseer—a traveling elder assigned by the country's branch office to a Circuit for three years, at which point he will rotate to a new Circuit. Analogous to a bishop. Visits each Congregation twice a year, for a week at a time. May be single or married. While ostensibly there to encourage local Witnesses, he is checking the level of preaching activity and donations, and generally keeping everyone toeing the company line. Also oversees the local Circuit Assemblies and Pioneer School. His living expenses are paid by the Congregations in the circuit; a vehicle and apartment are provided by JW headquarters.

Congregation—local group of around one hundred JWs. Several congregations may share one Kingdom Hall.

Convention—annual summer regional conference of at least several thousand JWs. Originally eight days long, but have gradually been shortened over the years to the current three days.

Counsel—a verb or noun meaning a session of verbal warning or reprimand based on Bible scriptures. "I counseled him about getting to meetings late." "The counsel was to study the Bible daily." Counsel may be given by anyone, to anyone below them: older kids to younger kids, elders to publishers, older sisters to younger sisters. Sisters would not counsel Brothers, and a young person would not counsel an adult, unless the youth held a position of authority—such as a Ministerial Servant to a non-Ministerial Servant.

Delete—to take away a Privilege for a perceived wrongdoing; synonym of "remove." "The Elder was deleted because his son went off to university."

Disassociation—the process of formally leaving the Organization voluntarily. Usually done by writing a letter to the local body of Elders.

Disfellowshipping—the process of expelling a member from the Congregation against their will for wrongdoing. Also called shunning. Analogous to "excommunication" for the Catholic church and Latter-day Saints, or "disconnection" for Scientology.

Elder—local Congregation ministers appointed by the Organization to lead the Congregation. Analogous to pastors or priests. They give talks, conduct Judicial Committees, and generally direct congregation activity. No set number; generally, between three and fifteen men make up the body of elders in each congregation. A man must be a Ministerial Servant for several years before being considered for an elder. It is unpaid, and most work secularly. Most are married and have children, but some are single.

Experience—an anecdote about preaching. "Wow, wasn't that a great experience in the new *Watchtower*?"

Field service/field ministry/or just "service"—the public preaching JWs do from door to door and on the street. Refers to the initial cold calls, as well as the Return Visits and Bible Studies with those that showed some interest. From Jesus' words at John 4:35, "[V]iew the fields, that they are white for harvesting."

Friends—a group of Congregation members. "The friends really enjoyed the Circuit Assembly."

Get-together—a party

Governing Body—the small group of men directing the JW Organization. No set number; generally ranges between eight and seventeen. They live and work at the Bethel world headquarters. All are required to be of the Anointed. Appointment lasts until death. Current members jointly appoint new members.

Great Crowd—all JWs who do not feel they are one of the 144,000 Anointed going to heaven; the vast majority of JWs. The great crowd expects to live forever in a paradise on earth, ruled over from heaven by Jesus and the 144,000. Also called the Other Sheep.

Hall—short for Kingdom Hall; another term for a Congregation. "There's a lot of older Friends in my hall."

Information board—the bulletin board in the Kingdom Hall where schedules and letters from headquarters are displayed.

Jehovah—the personal name of God. Jesus' father and creator, and a separate person from Jesus

Jesus—the son of Jehovah God. Unlike many Christian denominations, JWs do not teach the Trinity or that Jesus is God. They believe that Jesus was the first thing God created, his "only-begotten son." Subsequently, Jesus and Jehovah worked as a team to create everything else in the universe. Hence, Jesus is the second most powerful person in the universe, but subservient to Jehovah. Only Jehovah God is worshipped.

Judicial committee—a panel of three Elders convened in cases of serious wrongdoing, to decide the guilty party's punishment. Discipline ranges from a private reprimand up to expulsion via Disfellowshipping.

Kingdom Hall—the church building where Meetings are held twice a week.

Meeting—when JWs meet together for worship services. Currently there is a midweek meeting and a weekend meeting, each about two hours long. Various short Bible talks are given, JW videos may be shown, three songs are sung, two prayers are offered, and there are periods for the audience to give comments in a question-and-answer format.

Memorial, The—the annual springtime commemoration of Jesus' death. Similar to Catholic communion or Latter-day Saint sacrament, but held only once per year. Based on 1 Corinthians 11:23–26. An hour-long talk, during which matzo bread and red wine—the "emblems"—are passed around to all attendees. However, only the Anointed eat and drink. Considered the most important meeting of the year. The only holiday JWs observe.

Ministerial servant—men in the local Congregation appointed by the Organization to assist the Elders in congregation tasks. Analogous to deacons. They do various necessary jobs, such as the accounting, keeping literature in stock, and organizing coverage of the congregation's territory. Ministerial servants who are good at public speaking may also be assigned to give talks. It is unpaid, and they may be single or have families.

Missionary—historically, a graduate of the five-month training course called "Gilead." Approximately one hundred graduates per year. Assigned to a foreign country for the rest of their life. Preaches 130 hours per month. Housing is provided by the organization. Receive a stipend for expenses. Allowed a visit home every three years.

Organization, The—the JW leadership structure at Bethel world headquarters, as led by the Governing Body. Decides current JW doctrine and policies, which are announced primarily in the *Watchtower* magazine, as well as in frequent letters or directives to congregation Elders. Also called the Watchtower Society, or just the Society. See "Society."

Other Sheep—see Great Crowd

Pioneer—a Congregation member who pledges to spend a set number of hours each month preaching door to door, for a minimum of one year. Must be approved by the Elders first. Currently a Regular Pioneer is required to put in seventy hours per month. An Auxiliary Pioneer signs up for a single month of fifty hours. A Regular Auxiliary Pioneer is fifty hours, but continuously. Regular Pioneers are held in high esteem in the congregation. They have a special meeting with the Circuit Overseer during his visits. Invited to attend Pioneer School after their first year is completed.

Pioneer School—a class Regular Pioneers attend after completing their first year of pioneering. Currently six days long. Generally, two neighboring Circuits will combine to have one Pioneer School annually. The two Circuit Overseers are the instructors.

Place—a verb meaning to leave literature with someone. "I placed four magazines this morning." "Placements" is the noun. "I want to increase my placements this month."

Platform—the raised stage at the front of the hall, on which JWs stand (Brothers) or sit (Sisters) to give a Talk

Preaching—see "Field Service"

Privileges—the right to do various things at the Meetings, such as giving comments, giving Talks from the Platform, passing microphones. Can be taken away as discipline for wrongdoing.

Public Talk—the Sunday sermon given in the Kingdom Hall. Currently thirty minutes long. Talks are developed from approximately one hundred outlines containing talking points and source material. Outlines are created by the Organization. Public talks are given by local Elders and Ministerial Servants. Congregations also routinely exchange speakers with nearby congregations to add variety.

Publisher—a person approved by the Elders to go Preaching door to door after studying a JW textbook (usually for at least several months) with one of Jehovah's Witnesses. Children of JW parents are also expected to become publishers, generally around six years of age. Publishers initially are unbaptized, and eventually are expected to get baptized. Publishers are expected to at least match the national average of hours preaching, generally around ten per month. Low-hour-publishers are five hours or less. If an entire month goes by without preaching, the publisher is Irregular. If six months go by, they are Inactive. Infirm or elderly publishers may, if approved by the elders, put in only fifteen minutes per month and still be in good standing. Publishers are required to submit a report at the end of each month to the elders, noting how many hours were spent preaching, and the amount of literature placed or videos shown. These figures are recorded in a file kept on each publisher by the congregation's Elders, and are reviewed by the Circuit Overseer during his visits.

Reach out—to set a goal to attain a certain role or Privilege. "He's reaching out to become an Elder." From 1 Timothy 3:1

Remove—to take away a privilege from someone because of wrongdoing. "He was removed as a Pioneer for viewing pornography."

Reproof—a process of discipline for wrongdoing not requiring Disfellowshipping. Congregation responsibilities and Privileges are taken away. May be "private reproof" (done privately) or "public reproof" (announced to the congregation that So-and-so has been reproved for an unspecified offense).

Return visit—a person who had shown some interest, or accepted some literature, on the initial cold call. Their name, address, and any personal info one could use to continue the conversation is written down (if allowed by a country's privacy laws). In about a week, the publisher starts visiting the house again to try and make contact—the return visit—and every week or two after that, with the goal of starting a weekly Bible Study with them. Return visits may continue for years or until the householder says they're no longer interested. The return visit is the action, but also refers to the householder. "My return visit lives down the street." Also referred to as "calls." "Anyone have any calls they can do?" An abbreviated form of the archaic term "back-calls," as return visits were previously known. While not set in stone, morning Field Service often falls into a predictable pattern, wherein the first hour is spent in Preaching door to door, followed by a coffee break, and the second hour is spent doing return visits until noon. By strategically trying a return visit in one area, followed by a return visit at the other end of the Territory, et cetera, it is possible for a Car Group that was feeling lazy to pass an entire morning only visiting a handful of houses. Good for cold winter days.

Russell, Charles Taze—the founder of the Bible Students, who were later renamed Jehovah's Witnesses. The first president of the Society until his death in 1916.

Rutherford, Joseph—the second president of the Bible Students after Russell's death. The name Jehovah's Witnesses was adopted during his tenure. President from 1917 until his death in 1942.

Serve—to hold a particular role or position. "He served as a Ministerial Servant for three years."

Sister—the term JWs use to refer to female Witnesses. "Sister Smith," "Brother Jones."

Society, The—a term, now somewhat out of favor, signifying the Governing Body and the rest of headquarters staff, who live and work at the JW world headquarters in New York State, United States, and who set JW policy. Synonymous with "Organization." Short for "Watchtower Bible and Tract Society." JWs have, in the past few decades, endeavored to create separation between the men taking the spiritual lead—the Governing Body—and the legal corporations used by JWs. This, in theory, insulates them from legal repercussions. During World War I, Joseph Rutherford—the Society's president—and other members of the board of directors were sentenced to prison under anti-espionage laws. The idea is that this would be impossible today, since none of the Governing Body members hold corporation positions such as president, vice president, or treasurer. It has had curious consequences. For example, it allowed Governing Body member Gerrit Lösch to aver in 2014 that "I do not answer to Watchtower…Watchtower does not have, and never has had, any authority over me," in a document explaining why he would not appear for a deposition in a child abuse case. To the average JW, the Watchtower Society and the

Governing Body of Jehovah's Witnesses are the same thing, but Governing Body members are willing to use semantics if it helps them avoid appearing in court. At Matthew 10:18, Jesus told his disciples, "And you will be brought before governors and kings for my sake, for a witness to them and the nations." The Governing Body has shown a marked reticence to jump into that role.

Step down—to voluntarily resign from a privilege or position. "He stepped down from serving as an Elder for a few years."

Talk—a sermon

Territory—the set area of a city or county assigned to a Congregation to cover in door-to-door preaching.

Theocratic—an activity or arrangement that is in accord with JW doctrine. Based on the idea that God's one true organization is a theocracy, a government ruled by God.

Theocratic Ministry School—a now-discontinued public speaking course incorporated into one of the Congregation meetings. Every congregation member was enrolled, received periodic speaking assignments, and received feedback from one of the Elders.

The Truth—the complete body of JW doctrine; also, the organization as a whole. "When did you come in the truth?" "How did you learn the truth?" "She fell out of the truth."

Watchtower—can refer to the organization of Jehovah's Witnesses as a whole; short for Watchtower Bible and Tract Society. See "Society." Can also refer to the *Watchtower* magazine, the main journal JWs have published since 1879.

Witness—short for one of Jehovah's Witnesses. "I met some Witnesses on vacation." Also, a noun or verb meaning to

Preach, or to give a favorable impression of JWs by conduct alone. "By not wearing miniskirts, I give my classmates a good witness." "I'm going to witness to my new teacher this fall."

Worldly—everything not godly. JWs view everything in black-and-white, either/or terms. You're on God's side or Satan's. Since 1 John 5:19 says the whole world is in Satan's control, "worldly" carries a very negative connotation for JWs. It is used as the Amish use it, in the archaic sense. Worldly means everything nonbelievers do that true worshippers don't. Worldly music includes rap and heavy metal. Worldly clothing is revealing and tight. Worldly people include all non-JWs. The dictionary definition of worldly, meaning urbane or sophisticated, carries a neutral to positive connotation, but this sense of the word is unused among JWs. Such a person, well traveled and well versed in the world's customs, would be looked at with a vague suspicion by loyal JWs, and indeed it's uncommon for a well-educated individual to become one of JWs. On the rare occasion a scientist or entertainer converts, the religion will often proudly write an article about them.

Prologue

Dear Britta,

There's not much time. The enemy is closing in on our position, and the rattle of gunfire keeps getting louder. If we never see each other again, know this: in a right triangle, the length of one side squared times the other side squared equals the hypotenuse squared. It's the Pythagorean theorem, which is to say, you're all that and a bag of chips. You square my hypotenuse seven ways to Sunday. Have our paths diverged? Yes. Was *The Fault In Our Stars* a better Shailene Woodley film than *Divergent*? Also yes. You're one of Jehovah's Witnesses. I left...

Sorry, we had to change our location. It bought us a little more time, at the cost of one of our number. The world will never forget you, Don Cheadle. As I was saying, my leaving Jehovah's Witnesses put a rift in our friendship deeper than the Marianas Trench, which is 36,037 feet deep at its maximum depth. But we're tough little Chiquita bananas, albeit toughness is a rarely considered quality when selecting bananas. Growing up as a Witness gives a person a pretty thick skin, 2.36 times thicker than normal, which makes tanning difficult for us and explains the blindingly pale complexions you and I have. Why am I only writing you now, and not before the rifting? Hmmm. The riftosity? The riftening? Well, this is why.

☞

PROLOGUE

"You're **gutless.**

You're a **gutless wonder!"**

— Fran
Strictly Ballroom

And of course by "you," I mean me. I'm the gutless wonder. Before I'm hacked into pieces which will be variously mounted on a warlord's mantel, and ground up into a powerful aphrodisiac, I thought you should know that. I'm sorry I didn't explain my exit. I just assumed our friendship wouldn't survive, so I shut it down like a nuclear reactor having a core meltdown. I couldn't tilt your world that far, suddenly off-kilter, like a step one inch lower than where it's expected to be.

Now I wonder. Was I right? Or was it a mistake, like assuming *The China Syndrome* is real? Did I underestimate you, your capacity to grow and adapt, your love of truth? Not just JW truth, but truth so true it hurts, which had knocked me to my knees with its brutal honesty.

PROLOGUE

"So, do you want to take a **leap** of faith?"

-Mr. Saito, *Inception*

Dear Britta

Perhaps had I possessed a bit more faith, we could have made a leap together. Instead, I find I have a bit of dream Saito in me, an old man filled with regret. Which isn't entirely a bad thing. To regret nothing is to have learned nothing.

The mortars are raining down hard now, and we've taken cover under a bridge. Let's see, by the light of my Petzl headlamp, yes let's do that. Perhaps I can tell you how it is I lost my faith. Left the faith. And maybe, just maybe, you might begin to see what I saw. To, possibly, even come to teeter at the chasm's edge. Scary stuff. Unless. Unless you suddenly find, to your surprise, that you are not about to fall. You are about to take flight.

Should you get to experience that emotion, which I believe is referred to (in all the most reputable scientific literature) as joypanicreliefexcitementfearhappinessanticipation, I would be a happy man. I think I'd be more jazzed than Wynton Marsalis when *Blood on the Fields* won a Pulitzer Prize. But you know what, I think maybe we've both ceded enough of our lives to other people. Persons eager to tell us how to think. How to dress, how to behave, how to spend our time on this earth, our energy and our money. Telling us who we must *be*. So, chica, you do you. I'll do me. And perhaps the twain *shall* meet one of these days, lord willing and the creek don't rise.

More to follow.

Prologue

"I'm looking for a place to **start**

and everything feels so **different** now

just grab a hold of my **hand**

I will lead you through this **wonderland**"

- "Yellow Light"
Of Monsters and Men

Truth

I AM A LIAR. I SHOULD MENTION THAT STRAIGHTAWAY. ONE DAY when I was about thirteen, some other Jehovah's Witnesses and I were out preaching door to door.

"Where's Susannah today?" one of them asked. Susannah is my sister, two years younger.

"Oh, she's home sick with…cholera," I replied.

The words rolled easily off my lips. Truthfully, Susannah had a cold. Cholera probably came from some Louisa May Alcott book I was reading. Maybe from watching *Swiss Family Robinson*. (Or was it plague in that movie?) Point was, the lie came easy. I guess I'd meant it as a joke. But I omitted the part where I fessed up. That afternoon, my confused parents began getting calls from friends concerned Susannah lay at death's door.

My religion preached scrupulous honesty. The literature teems with anecdotes of Witnesses being lauded by the community for their honest actions. The phrase "the truth" has come to be shorthand for referring to the religion as a whole. "When did they come into the truth?" "Were you raised in the truth, or did you learn the truth as an adult?" "It's so sad, she fell out of the truth."

But for Witnesses, transparency is not the same thing as honesty. The organizational structure is built on layers of confidentiality. When my dad was appointed a congregation minister—which JWs call elders—he was issued a handbook titled *Shepherd the Flock of God*. It's three hundred pages of rules governing behavior in the congregation. Access to its contents is restricted to elders only. Rank-and-file members are forbidden to read it. Yet, they are obligated to follow its rules. It's like getting pulled over for speeding in a town which has no speed limit signs posted. Trust me, the officer says, you were over the limit.

***

"Where are you headed?" the border patrol officer asked me.

"Oh, Fort Erie," I replied. I was crossing from Buffalo into Canada.

"And what is the purpose of your visit?"

"I'm going to Tim Hortons." Sure, it's a perfectly fine coffee shop, but do you really need to drive to Canada for coffee?

"I see...and how long will you be staying?"

"Just a couple of hours." I had a bike in my trunk, and was meeting a guy who wanted to buy it. He asked me to bring it into Canada, so he wouldn't have to pay any taxes. I wasn't exactly sure whether I was doing something illegal, but it sure felt like it.

"You're driving two hours to get a coffee at Tim Hortons?" The officer's skepticism was palpable. A bead of sweat trickled down my forehead. I wasn't lying to a federal agent, I told myself. I was just omitting pertinent information.

"Of course, being **truthful** does **not** mean that we are obligated to divulge all information to anyone who asks it of us."

- *Awake* 02/08/00 p. 21

Truth

I saw a faint glimmer of hope, a sliver of wiggle room in which I wouldn't be lying, while still not telling the truth.

"Oh, no, I'm not coming from Jamestown. I'm just driving from Holiday Valley," I replied. It was a nearby ski resort I'd been working at earlier in the day. The agent relaxed.

"Is that right? I love Holiday Valley!" he said. A minute later he waved me through, and I was on my mildly felonious way.

***

"Thus the Scriptures show that for the purpose of protecting the interests of God's cause, it is proper to

hide the **truth**

from God's enemies...

This would come under the term

'war strategy,'

as explained in *The Watchtower*, February 1, 1956".

- *Watchtower* 06/01/60 p. 352

I grew up versed in this "war strategy." It wasn't in the same league as the Fair Game tactics of Scientology, but speaking half-truths? Wholly acceptable. What someone didn't know wouldn't hurt them. I'd learned it was how Witnesses outwitted the Nazis in World War II. Heck, Jesus himself withheld information from his opposers. Really, I had only one concern about the tactic: would I be strong enough to match the steely resolve of earlier JWs?

During a traveling minister's visit to our congregation, he regaled us one lunch hour with stories of persecution. I was transfixed as he described how officials in one country had repeatedly whipped a girl on the soles of her feet. This, he gravely explained to us kids sitting around him on the floor, was because the bottoms of the feet are packed with nerve endings, making them exquisitely sensitive to pain. That tracked. I'd stepped on LEGOs. Yet, despite the torture, she wouldn't give up the names of other Witnesses she knew. I made a brief attempt to start going around barefoot after that, to toughen up my feet.

I am a liar.

Half-truths and omissions characterized our preaching door to door. Sometimes people would ask, do you believe only Jehovah's Witnesses will be saved? The FAQs on the JW website flatly answer, no. On the doorstep, I'd always give a cagey answer that, well, only God can judge people's hearts. But among Witnesses, the answer is obviously yes. It's pretty much the whole point of being in the religion.

"Only Jehovah's Witnesses,

    those of the anointed remnant and the 'great crowd,'

        as a united organization under the protection of the Supreme Organizer,

have any scriptural hope of surviving

    the impending end of this doomed system dominated by Satan the Devil."

— *Watchtower* 09/01/89 p. 19, par. 7

***

"How is my son?" she asked.

Her eyes sought me, sliding impossibly far to the right, until there was almost more white than pupil showing. Her neck was immobilized in a cervical brace, so that her head was forced to stare up at the ceiling. Her hand searched blindly for mine. Dried blood was smeared across her fingers. She clutched my gloved hand fiercely.

The woman had been in a brutal car wreck, t-boned by a drunk driver. She had been fortunate, emerging with some broken bones and scrapes, but nothing needing immediate surgery. I would be her nurse in the intensive care unit.

"Do you know what happened to my son?" she repeated. He had been on the passenger side, which had taken the brunt of the impact. He was a high school senior, a likeable kid, I would learn, who was going to be salutatorian.

Except he was dead.

***

Being a nurse is a weird intersection of power and impotence. Nurses are a dime a dozen to hospitals, essential yet underappreciated cogs in the healthcare machine. However, before almost anyone else, they know test results which may forever change a person's life. Whether someone is pregnant, had a stroke, needs surgery, has cancer, is going to die. Nurses withhold most of that information, doling it out to patients in small amounts which vary randomly from nurse to nurse. I know that probably sounds bad, but it's not really. You don't want to find out you have cancer in passing as your nurse empties your bedpan. You want to hear it from a physician who is ready with game plans and options and answers to unanswerable questions.

I knew her son had been killed at the scene. The ambulance crew had passed it on to the emergency department, who had passed it on to me. But no one wanted to tell this poor woman with her in this state: lying flat on her back, alone in the room, staring up at the ceiling tiles. Family was on the way, police said.

I leaned far over the bed to meet her eyes, and they pleaded with me, wanting the answer she perhaps already suspected. I debated internally. On the one hand, I had no problem invoking the JW "war strategy" of withholding information. That's what everyone else had done so far. On the other hand, her son dying meant little to me. Witnesses believe virtually everyone now dead will soon be resurrected for a second go-round here on earth. It gave me a fatalistic, pragmatic outlook. What was the big deal if someone died? It was about as serious as pausing a movie. But on the third hand, I hated giving bad news. And family was on the way.

I am a liar.

"I'm not sure, but I'll find out about your son," I told her. "Right now, I need to get you settled." My lie did little to quiet her fears, but it bought a few minutes until her family arrived. They rushed past me into her room, and a moment later came the anguished wail I was braced for. It's a gut-wrenching sound which, gratefully, isn't heard too often in the ICU. When it does occur, a silence falls over the unit for a moment. There is a rapid flicker of eyes from one ICU nurse to another, like flashes of electricity. It is the acknowledgement of defeat. We are there to fix people, to save lives. But we cannot fix this. There is no medication I can push, or pillow I can adjust, to make it all better.

***

"Satan, 'the father of the lie,'

uses

those under

his control to spread

lies

about Jehovah and about

our brothers and

sisters."

- *Watchtower* 11/19 p.15, par. 8

Dear Britta

Jehovah's Witnesses exist in a binary world. I always liked it, because it was simple. Anyone not actively working for Jehovah God is working for Satan the Devil. Easy. And I guess that includes me now, now that I've left the religion behind. So let me just put at ease anyone reading this, particularly any Witnesses. Perhaps you'll read something in this book which strikes you as doubtful, disturbing, hard to accept. In those moments, reassure yourself. Remember: I am a liar. That is the truth.

Bethel

I've taken a lot of trips to Bethel over the years. Beth-El, a Hebrew word translated as "House of God," is what Jehovah's Witnesses call their headquarters complexes. In the days of Joseph Rutherford, the second president of the religion ultimately named Jehovah's Witnesses and of its corporate structure—the Watch Tower Bible and Tract Society of Pennsylvania—they also had Beth-Sarim, "House of the Princes." A San Diego, California house constructed for Rutherford in 1929, Beth-Sarim had ten bedrooms—ostensibly for Bible characters such as Abraham and Moses to live in once they were resurrected. In the meantime, Rutherford very kindly acted as caretaker. He wintered there each year with his retinue, until his death on the property in 1942.

As World War II started in 1939, Beth-Shan—"House of Security"—was built on an adjacent seventy-five-acre lot in San Diego. In 1926, the Watch Tower Society's *Golden Age* magazine (now called *Awake*) explained what would probably happen in the next war.

"The compact, thickly-populated, highly industrialized centers of civilization will be **drenched** with gases, bathed with **liquid-fire** and sown with **bacteria**.

Unquenchable **conflagrations** will overspread the sky with a blanket of smoke, almost impenetrable to light, hiding the **orbs** of day and night and the constellations, reacting on the human mind to **plunge** it into hopelessness and **gloom**.

Perhaps some previous preparation will have been made of elaborate **subterranean** tunnels and chambers in anticipation of this **awful** time."

- Golden Age 06/02/26, p. 551

Rutherford had evidently become a bit concerned about the war, so Beth-Shan added a few features missing from Beth-Sarim. Workers constructed an airstrip inside the compound, in case access by road became cut off. A sturdy gate was erected, which protected an orchard, space for residents to grow their own crops, and a sizable water storage tank. Perhaps the key feature was a hidden underground bomb shelter, accessed by pulling a lever inside a bathroom medicine cabinet. Eighty years later, only Beth-El remains as a JW property. Beth-Sarim and Beth-Shan were quietly sold off after World War II came and went without the *Golden Age*'s comments coming to pass. Abraham, Isaac, and Jacob never did show up in San Diego to claim their bedrooms.

When I was a kid, my congregation organized bus trips to all the U.S. Bethel sites every year or two. Since they were all concentrated in New York State, many East Coast congregations did that. It was like our own little pilgrimage to Mecca. These trips were typically whirlwind three-day events; we lived in Rochester, New York—about six hours away. (Each country's branch office is called Bethel. This includes the United States branch, but the U.S. Bethel is also the world headquarters.)

The usual itinerary was: visit Brooklyn Bethel in New York City (which in those days housed the world headquarters and did book printing); the JW-owned Stanley Theater in New Jersey (a beautifully restored 1920s theater used for assemblies); Watchtower Farms in Wallkill, New York (which did magazine printing and some actual farming); and the Watchtower Educational Center in Patterson, New York (the site of classrooms for various JW courses, audio/video production, and the art department).

In 1881, the Watch Tower Society was created in Pittsburgh, Pennsylvania. However, the Society eventually set its sights on New

York City. Brooklyn was informally known as "The City of Churches," and it was hoped the location change would help the sermons of Charles Russell—the religion's founder—to be syndicated in more newspapers. And it worked, boosting the number from eleven to two thousand. Additionally, the nascent religion was eager to forget Russell's messy and very public divorce proceedings, which Pittsburgh newspapers had closely followed.

The first New York City properties they bought are an interesting story in and of themselves. In the mid-1800s, Henry Ward Beecher was a popular preacher with close ties to the Lincoln administration. (Beecher's sister was Harriet Beecher Stowe, author of *Uncle Tom's Cabin*.) Russell's senior by forty years, Beecher was known nationwide until his death in 1887. He was, perhaps, the Billy Graham of the Civil War era.

When it was learned in 1908 that Beecher's former home and a mission building from his Plymouth Church were for sale in Brooklyn, the Watch Tower Society—keen to build more legitimacy among its religious peers—quickly purchased the properties. And why the name Bethel? The former mission building had been called the Beecher Bethel. Although Russell had called his Pittsburgh headquarters "Bible House" for nineteen years, he decided to drop that name in New York City and stick with the Plymouth Church's moniker of Bethel. And Bethel it has been ever since.

The Watch Tower Society operated out of Brooklyn for more than a century. In order to provide oversight for the steady influx of new members in the twentieth century and keep up with the growing demand for printed literature, the small two-building operation of 1908 expanded considerably over the years. Many smaller properties were purchased over the years, but some real estate deals were especially notable. In 1969 Watchtower bought a complex of ten buildings from E.R. Squibb and Sons (who would later become the pharmaceutical giant Bristol-Myers Squibb), which added 600,000 ft^2 of office and factory space. In 1983, a property purchase at 360 Furman Street added 1,000,000 ft^2 for shipping operations and other services. By 1995, a thirty-story residence building had been constructed at 90 Sands Street. At the peak, more than three thousand Bethelites worked in Brooklyn.

However, it seems the terrorist attacks of September 11, 2001 may have rattled JW leadership. They had already been learning, over the years, not only the perks of being headquartered in New York City, but the drawbacks. Expansion was difficult and expensive. Every construction project needed approval from multiple city departments and community groups. And logistically, things had evolved. The Internet was making it less important to be located in a major shipping hub. The terrorist attacks were the icing on the cake, and shortly afterward the organization began laying plans to move its headquarters out of New York City.

It took well over a decade to sell off its considerable property portfolio, but by 2017 the process was more or less complete. The printeries and brownstones of Brooklyn Heights were replaced by a shiny new complex near Warwick, New York, an hour outside the city. Brooklyn property values had risen nicely over the decades. According to state records, the organization pocketed $2 billion from the various transactions. Now that's a lot of chimichangas.

As of 2019, Jehovah's Witnesses have eighty-nine branch offices around the world, staffed by approximately 20,000 volunteers. The organization doesn't break down that number by country, but it appears that between two and three thousand Witnesses currently work at the three main United States complexes of Warwick, Wallkill, and Patterson. Akin to the Sea Org of Scientology,

Bethelites agree to work full-time in exchange for food and housing. They are paid about ninety-five cents per hour. It is an astonishingly low figure, but many JWs are eager to sign up, because Bethel is the spiritual center of the organization.

The bus trips we took to NYC were in the pre-iPad days, so I remember a lot of sing-alongs during the drive. The selections were always JW-composed religious songs, known as Kingdom Melodies. At seven or eight years old, my sister Susannah and I favored volume over technique. One time the Witness in front of us turned around, clearly annoyed. "Good voices!" she said through gritted teeth, as we yelled another song in her ears.

The visits were great, and they fueled my ultimate goal: living and working (or "serving," as it's termed) at Bethel. That was going to be my thing. Everything about it was thrilling—how spotless the production floors were, the speed of the printing presses, the idea that at any moment you could come face to face with a Governing Body member. (The Governing Body is the group of about a dozen men—there's no set number—who direct and control the entire JW religion, much as the Church of Jesus Christ of Latter-day Saints—the Mormons—have their First Presidency and Quorum of the Twelve Apostles.)

One year my dad used a week of his vacation time to help on one of the never-ending Watchtower construction projects in Brooklyn. He loved telling the story of how he'd been working with an electrical crew, when a Governing Body member (I forget now which one) walked by them and quipped, "Make way for these men! They have the power!"

When I was probably about ten, a young guy from our hall named John applied and was accepted to Brooklyn Bethel. He was always friendly, and I'd write to him (using Bethel stationery I'd bought on previous bus trips) asking all about what it was like there. (One of my top concerns: what if you're running a press and have to go to the bathroom?)

A couple of years later, I met Max Larson at an assembly. (Assemblies are larger, regional gatherings of JWs held a few times a year.) Max had been the factory overseer at Brooklyn Bethel for many years, and eventually became the vice president of the Watchtower Society's New York corporation. His autobiography was published in the *Watchtower* magazine right around that time, which was fascinating reading for me. Now I found myself face to face with the man himself. I nervously said *I* wanted to work at Bethel when I was older. He peered at me from under untamed eyebrows that had never seen a trimmer. After what seemed like an eternity, he said, "Okay, I'm saving you a spot." I was elated. (Didn't think to get it in writing, though.)

Around thirteen years old, I asked my friend Ryan what he wanted to be when he grew up. "A marine biologist," he replied nonchalantly. That threw me for a loop. You were supposed to have a JW goal: Bethelite, missionary (preacher in a foreign country), or circuit overseer (a sort of regional manager of twenty congregations). Those were the choices. I think he could tell I was surprised, and asked what I wanted to do. "Go to Bethel," I said firmly. It would be worth signing the required Vow of Poverty. I would be at the hub of it all. You could keep your Jerusalem, your Mecca and Vatican City. I knew the truth: Brooklyn was the most spiritual place on earth.

"Nor are Scriptural vows to be compared with the **so-called** 'monastic vows' that persons in later centuries were required to make in order to gain admittance into certain ***religious orders of church organizations.*** Those **vows of 'chastity, poverty and obedience'** placed those vowing under obligation to the religious orders and served those orders as a means of **exercising control** over their adherents."

- *Watchtower* 10/01/73, p. 607

"Today, there are about 67,000 members of the ***Worldwide Order of Special Full-Time Servants of Jehovah's Witnesses...*** Each of them has made a **'Vow of Obedience and Poverty.'** In this vow, they promise to work hard at **any assignment they are given** in Jehovah's service".

- *Watchtower* 04/17, p. 9, par. 19

Bethel

Time passed, and I began pioneering after graduating high school. (Pioneering means agreeing to preach door to door a minimum number of hours per month, for at least one year. It was ninety hours per month at the time, since reduced to seventy.) If you wanted to be accepted to Bethel at the minimum age of nineteen, you needed to be a pioneer. It was competitive; there were more applicants than openings.

Soon, my peers started to go to Bethel. One guy I knew, Jim, went off to Brooklyn. But he returned home just a year later under mysterious circumstances. The first year is probationary, and he wasn't invited to stay on.

"It is expected that all who become members of the Bethel family will have **long ago** stopped any **unclean,** *filthy* **habits** or unscriptural practices that they might have engaged in prior to learning **the truth**".

- *Dwelling Together in Unity* p. 22

Unlike my reserved self, my sister Susannah was outgoing and made friends easily. (While we were out preaching, she'd often pose questions to the group such as, if you were a doughnut, what kind would you be?) She knew lots of young Bethelites, most of whom I'm guessing were hoping to go out with her. (Bethelites tend to be a thirsty bunch. A classic joke JWs tell describes a father putting a Bible, a Barbie doll, and a beer bottle in front of his baby son. The item his son grabbed would signify the direction his adult life would take. A Bible means a spiritual man. A Barbie doll indicates a womanizer. And the beer bottle, a lush. The father rushes to a mentor in a panic. "He picked up all three! What does that mean?" His friend gets a knowing look on his face. "Ah, he is going to be a Bethelite.")

Sometimes Susannah and I would drive down to visit Bethelites we knew, or if one of them had a car, they'd come visit us. We saw a wide range of living quarters at Bethel, and the variety was intriguing. New guys would get cramped bedrooms with bathrooms down the hall. Longtime Bethelites score large apartments with attached living rooms and bathrooms. Residents bid for better rooms as they become available. It all goes by seniority—that is, your years of full-time service (pioneering and Bethel combined). If a kid started pioneering at twelve years old, as a few eager beavers do, he could conceivably enter Bethel with seven years of seniority. The lucky dog would end up with a pretty sweet room right off the bat. (I'm guessing everyone else hates those guys, but as Doris Day sang out, que será, será.)

Particularly in Brooklyn, some rooms had great views of the New York City skyline. When one young guy we knew had us up to his place, we found a huge space with a stunning view of the city. As we looked out the windows, he explained how his roommate was a real weirdo, but that the guy had over twenty years of seniority. It bummed me out. He was pretending to be this guy's friend simply to get the great apartment. Naively, I'd just assumed being a Bethelite automatically meant you were a great person.

My friend Eric went off to Watchtower Farms. I was really bad at staying in touch. (I'm still terrible. Sorry, all my friends I never contact! I miss you!) Fortunately, a mutual friend called him regularly. He told me that reading between the lines, Eric was pretty unhappy at Bethel that first year. That simply didn't compute. How could you be unhappy…at *Bethel*? But he was really homesick. Especially there at Wallkill, local congregations are saturated with Bethelites. Many stay a couple of years and then move on. Local Witnesses don't have much incentive to make close friendships.

And for the first time, I began to consider the downsides of going to Bethel. It is a highly regimented life, rather like joining the military. I enjoyed my relative freedom as a pioneer. As long as I had my required preaching hours in by month end, I could do more or less as I pleased. Did I actually *want* to live in a dorm with communal bathrooms, having to be at breakfast each morning by 7:00 am, eating whatever was served, following strict rules about what to wear and how to behave? (New Bethelites are issued a handbook with thirty-some pages of rules, titled *Dwelling Together in Unity*. They also attend mandatory orientation courses called "Bethel Entrants School." And those are just the *written* rules.) I loved giving talks at congregation meetings each week. But with so many Bethelites in the area, I heard you were doing well to give a talk every six months.

	Yes	No
"Do you listen to music that features sexual immorality, violence, spiritism, profanity, or other subject matter inappropriate for a Christian?	☐	☐
In the past year, have you viewed material inappropriate for Christians, such as movies or videos featuring violence, spiritism, or sexual immorality? Or pornography in printed form, on the Internet, or otherwise?	☐	☐
Have you ever had a homosexual relationship? If you answer yes, please explain:"_____	☐	☐

— Bethel Application, A-8-E, 10/15

Unexpectedly, I began to get cold feet about applying. However, I continued attending the annual Bethel meeting at each summer convention. The meeting was for anyone interested in going; you could even apply on the spot. I can't tell you why I was still attending. I probably could have given the talk for them, I'd heard it so many times. But I never got up the nerve to walk to the front of the room and put pen to paper.

One day I decided: I definitively was not going to Bethel. I went out and put five hundred dollars down to buy a car. It was a boxy little Scion xB, if anyone remembers those. I loved it. Another crucial point—it had four doors. Any Witness who buys a two-door car is almost automatically considered a bad influence, because it isn't practical for taking a group preaching.

But the very next day, I called the dealer in a panic to back out. I lost my deposit. The thing was, if I bought the car, it meant—once and for all—I wasn't going to Bethel. You sure couldn't have a car payment on the small stipend you got working there. And I just couldn't close that door. Not yet.

I finally decided I ought to at least dip my toe in the water. As my mom always said, you can't say you don't like a food unless you take at least one bite. I applied to go for two weeks as a temporary worker, as my dad had done years before. Assigned to Watchtower Farms, I made the six-hour drive down, super nervous about everything. Eric was essentially the only person I knew there. I felt better that at least my roommate would be in the same boat. But then I met him. As it turned out, he had been a Bethelite there for years before getting married. He hooked up with his old buddies, and I never saw him again after the first day. It was a letdown, although I did get the room to myself.

I went down to breakfast early the next morning. To my dismay they explained that in the summertime, there were no assigned seats. Since so many Bethelites were away traveling, they closed part of the dining room. "Just sit wherever you like!" said the attendant.

My eyes scanned the room as I had flashbacks to grade school—having to walk up to a table of strangers and ask to sit with them. I didn't want to accidentally take a full-timer's seat. What had happened to the part where Bethel would tell me what to do every minute? Somehow, I stumbled into an empty chair. Looking back now, the mealtimes for those two weeks are a complete blank. It was an introvert's nightmare, and apparently I buried the memory deep in my brain's Pit of Despair.

Having no particular skills on tap, I was assigned to a demolition crew tearing down some cabins. It was hot work in the humid June weather. By the time I returned home, all my underwear had turned blue. I'd sweated all the dye out of my brand-new work jeans.

I enjoyed the hard labor, but I had no knack for making small talk as I worked. I would run wheelbarrow loads of debris to a dumpster until everything was cleaned up and then stop, at a loss what to do. The young guy overseeing the crew admonished me for standing around too much. I felt confused and out of sorts. My JW training had always been to do exactly what I was told and not overstep that one iota. Initiative was not rewarded. But it didn't quite work on a job site.

"We can save ourselves and others much *anxiety* and *grief* if we modestly **make decisions *only*** when we have been **granted** the authority to do so."

- *Watchtower* 04/15/11, p. 15, par. 11

I didn't seem to be meshing with my workmates at all. I wasn't super surprised. To some extent, thriving as a Witness means integrating with the group and picking up on unspoken cues. It was a skill that somehow I'd never been able to get the hang of. I knew Bible minutiae ninety-five percent of the population didn't, but I didn't know much about how to relate to others.

"I know everybody on this island,

seems

so

happy

on this island

everything is by
design

I know everybody on this island has a
role
on this island

so

maybe
I can roll with

mine"

— "How Far I'll Go"
Moana

All in all, it was a relief when my two weeks were up at Bethel. I shelved, for good, my plans to apply for a permanent spot. I reconsidered the three options I had in life as a JW. Bethelite? No. Circuit overseer? I liked giving talks, but the actual overseer-ing part of the job sounded awful. Missionary? You had to be married for that. Plus, I wasn't so great preaching door to door.

By that time, the organization had created a fourth option. I could apply to Ministerial Training School (MTS). It was a two-month Bible course for single men, and at the end I'd be assigned to a congregation in the United States which lacked enough guys to handle all the tasks. (There might be plenty of women in a congregation, but only the men are allowed to work in a leadership role.) MTS was probably the closest fit for me, but I still held back. I knew from the Bethel application that they would ask whether I dabbled with pornography. I did, despite my best intentions. I was a dabbler. Sometimes I dabbled myself several times a week. (I may have fudged those details on my Bethel application.) And it would mean moving to a whole new congregation of strangers. The thought made me break out in a cold sweat.

I hemmed and hawed, and in the end I didn't really do anything. I continued pioneering, more or less. But pioneering had always just been a stepping-stone to Bethel. My heart wasn't really in it. I often missed the monthly hour requirement, and eventually I was asked—to be frank, told—to stop and leave the ranks of pioneers. I felt the weight of my failures growing heavier.

I was uncomfortable moving forward with any of the approved JW goals, but those were the only options I could pick from. Eventually I came up with one thing I could do: sink into a deep depression. At last, something I was good at! And that's where things stayed for a while.

Maybe I'll leave it there for now. I don't want to go all Debbie Downer on you. A postscript: later I heard that my friend Ryan—whose goal had been to become a marine biologist—ended up going to Bethel, where he stayed for many years. He adopted my goal; perhaps I should have adopted his. I'd probably need to work on my swimming first.

Entertainment

SATURDAY WAS MOVIE NIGHT AT THE KUCHMANS. YOU COULD generally find the four of us sitting on my parents' king size bed, watching films on VHS. In those prehistoric days, we'd also rent the VCR—which seemed to weigh more than I did—along with the videotapes. We'd order takeout from two or three restaurants. After my dad picked it all up, we'd eat it together on the bed during the movie.

For many years, no movies with even a single curse word were allowed. Sex and violence even less so. No *Gone With the Wind* for us—that "I don't give a damn" was a deal breaker. On the other hand, it meant we watched a lot of the classics. The Marx brothers, Fred Astaire and Ginger Rogers, Gene Kelly, Katharine Hepburn, Jimmy Stewart—all the greats.

It also meant my movie knowledge had some big holes. I didn't watch *Star Wars* until my mid-teens. One time at a going away party for a family moving to Indiana, I was supposed to play Indiana Jones (get it?) in a skit. We did a lot of skits back then. But I'd never seen the *Indiana Jones* films, and didn't have the foggiest idea what his character was. Someone gave me a fedora to wear; that was as close as I got.

As I got older, the rules loosened up a little bit, and Susannah and I were allowed to watch PG movies. Once in a while, even PG-13! Oh yeah, we were two wiilllld and crazy [kids]! (Cue Steve Martin chest wiggle.)

I used a Christian movie review website I'd found to decide what would be okay to see. It reviewed movies, not in the sense of how artistically great a film was, but in terms of how much of it would be offensive to good Christians. So *Father of the Bride*, for example, would probably get an A+, whereas *The Godfather*—ooh, sorry, thanks for playing. The site listed how many times each swear word was used, what types of violence appeared, and how far each love scene went. (Now that I think about it, reading the detailed description of each sexy scene probably wasn't much more chaste than just watching the thing. Hey, I was trying.)

The one thing definitely off-limits was anything with magic, spiritism, or the occult. That was the problem with *Star Wars* (the concept of balance in the Force was too close to Chinese yin and yang philosophy), *Indiana Jones* (the guy getting his face melted from the spirits in the Ark of the Covenant), and obviously *The Wizard of Oz* (hello, witches).

I remember a group of us Witnesses going to see the movie *Anastasia*. It was a G-rated animated movie, a pretty innocuous choice for a nineteen-year-old. And then Rasputin the sorcerer came onto the screen. We all looked down the row at each other, and as one unit tromped back out of the theater. Just when you thought you were safe.

To be honest, Disney movies are usually minefields, because so many fairy tales have a magical character. From *Cinderella* to *Snow*

White to *Aladdin* to *The Little Mermaid*, they were all off the table. Some JWs didn't have such a strict no-magic policy, but my parents always erred on the side of caution. They were the original Muggles.

One could say that instead of cautionary fairy tales, JWs have cautionary Bible stories to keep little kids scared straight. The tales remind me of Greek mythology. There's lots of sex, violence, and familial infighting. As I read them now, I notice that Jehovah God takes the place of the bogeyman found in fairy tales. It's like he is Mother Teresa and a Mafia hit man all rolled into one.

Here's a typical passage from *My Book of Bible Stories*, the classic JW book for little children. It's Story 62: "Trouble in David's House" (not to be confused with *Big Trouble in Little China*). We pick it up after King David rapes Bathsheba ("makes love to her," as the book cheerfully puts it), gets her pregnant, and has her husband killed. (A kid who hasn't learned all about "making love" by the ripe old age of five clearly is slacking on his developmental milestones.)

"Jehovah says:
   'Because you have done these
bad things,
you will have a

lot of trouble in your house.'

And what trouble David has!

First, Bathsheba's son dies.

Then David's firstborn son Amnon gets his
sister Tamar alone and **forces** his

David's *love* on her.
son Absalom is so **angry**
about this that he **kills** Amnon.

Later,
Absalom wins the favor of many of the people,
and he has himself made **king**.

Finally, David wins the war
against Absalom, who is

killed.

Yes, David has a lot of trouble."

— "Trouble in David's House"
My Book of Bible Stories

I mean, I don't think it's the type of content you'd find in Amazon's top-selling children's books. But then again *Hansel and Gretel* had kids dumped in the forest and people shoved into ovens, so maybe it's all of a piece. I honestly really liked the *Bible Stories* book when I was little. It had lots of exciting pictures.

One of my favorite illustrations was Jael hammering a tent stake into Sisera's skull, the blood trickling down his temple (Story 50, "Two Brave Women"). I see they've omitted that image from the online *Bible Stories* book for some reason. Another was Queen Jezebel, with her crazy eyeshadow, getting pushed out of a window to be trampled by horses and eaten by dogs (Story 66, "Jezebel—A Wicked Queen"). And how about Solomon with his natty mustache telling his guard to cut a baby in half (Story 63, "Wise King Solomon"). I know it sounds like I'm cherry-picking all the violent pictures, but I seriously loved reading all these stories with my mom and dad. It was like the preschooler version of some salacious tabloid you can't stop buying.

Who can forget Story 20, "Dinah Gets Into Trouble." In this morality tale, Dinah befriends some Canaanites, and is raped by Shechem ("violated her," as Jehovah's Witnesses' *New World Translation* euphemistically puts it at Genesis 34:2).

The lesson that might be expected—respect women, rape is bad—is passed over in favor of a different one: hang out with the wrong crowd, and you have only yourself to blame if something bad happens. Got raped? Hey, you were asking for it going to *that* party! Or as the book puts it, "How did all this trouble get started? It was because Dinah made friends with people who did not obey God's laws."

"Although authorities cite many factors as the cause, some experts maintain that 'by their *seductive* behavior in dress, bodily movement and *suggestive* remarks, some women invite rape.'

(*The Globe and Mail*, Toronto, Canada)"

- *Awake* 07/22/86, p. 29

ENTERTAINMENT

"Don't send mixed messages. **Avoid** flirting or dressing **provocatively.** Such actions may send the **message** that you're interested in **getting physical** or at least that you **wouldn't object** to it."

- Questions Young People Ask, Answers That Work Vol. 1, p. 229

"If
a woman
or
a young girl
wears
very short dresses
and
tight, revealing clothing,
how
can
she
object
to being treated like
a loose woman,
since
that is often the way
prostitutes
dress?"

 — *Awake* 01/08/68 p. 22

ENTERTAINMENT

"Womankind must share the **blame...** actresses must also share in the **blame** for the increase in **rapes,** for after men have seen them on the screen they **frequently** go out and attack a woman who may be a paragon of virtue."

— *Awake* 03/08/74, p. 15

Hmm, I may have gone off on a bit of a tangent there. Back to movies. A favorite for me has always been *Contact*, with Jodie Foster. She plays a particular type of protagonist I loved as a JW: the quirky—but secretly great—loner who struggles to fit in with society. Can't imagine why I identified with that type of character. Other movies I liked along that line: *Jump Tomorrow* (filmed near me!); *Amelie* (after I allowed myself to start watching R-rated movies); *Ida* (subtitles, watch out); and *Strictly Ballroom*.

I don't remember which came first, reading Carl Sagan's book *Contact* or watching the movie. I loved the message of humankind working together to achieve a positive goal: to learn more about the universe, aided by benevolent beings off-world. It spoke to how I pictured my eternity in paradise.

(A crash course in JW theology: they believe that any day now, Armageddon will start. In this climactic war between human governments and God, all bad people will be destroyed. The good people (i.e., JWs) will survive and live forever in an idyllic paradise on earth. Witnesses don't believe in an immortal soul. Instead, they teach that since most people who died down through history never had the chance to learn about Jehovah, those people will be resurrected back to life here on earth after Armageddon, whereupon they will have the opportunity to become a worshiper of Jehovah. Or die. No pressure.)

Once in paradise, I figured I would spend a few millennia studying the earth. But after that, I wanted to travel through space, learning everything about everything. The Bible is silent on the matter of visiting other planets and faster-than-light travel after Armageddon. I had to speculate about what we'd be able to do.

"If one really wanted to get around and see things safely and conveniently in outer space, it would be wiser to follow Jesus' counsel and keep on seeking first God's Kingdom rather than to plan on becoming a space traveler in outer space ships. Those who inherit the heavenly kingdom will see *far more* than the things in outer space. They will get around with greater speed, angelic speed, and with more ease and convenience."

- *Watchtower* 11/15/59, p. 692, par. 3

I don't think I ever read that article. As a kid, I even looked into attending NASA's Space Camp. There were two problems. One, it was expensive, and two, JW kids just don't go to summer camp—too many bad influences there.

When I homeschooled, I picked aerospace as my science focus one year. (The curriculum was a lot more freeform than I imagine it is today.) Basically, I read a lot of library books about planes and flight. I liked to build and fly model rockets. I'd sit at the workbench in our basement, gluing rocket fins on with epoxy, while my Evanescence CD played on repeat.

But that was about all I could do. Being outside the public school system, I was struggling to teach myself basic math, never mind the calculus required for a career in aerospace. (Don't get me wrong though, I loved homeschooling. What kid would pass up a chance to not have to go to school?) Not to mention I knew a job like that would be full-time. JW jobs should be part-time or bust, baby! Gotta keep the schedule open for that sweet, sweet preaching work. Ah well, cleaning offices is pretty much as good as being a rocket scientist. Or at least, so I was told by elders in their talks at the meetings. And many of them *were* office cleaners, so they should know. (Each congregation generally has anywhere from three to fifteen elders, the JW equivalent of a pastor or priest.)

Another Carl Sagan book I've been reading lately is *The Demon-Haunted World*. In it, he debunks a lot of the pseudoscience which seems to periodically get popular. He points out that in the past, people feared demons and witches. Nowadays, people fear alien abduction, which probably all amounts to the same thing.

"What *wonderful*

unseen powers

are in the air
about us,

electric currents of all sorts,

magnetism,

heat,

radioactivity,

the spiritual powers of demonism

and

the beneficent powers of the holy angels".

— *Golden Age*
11/12/1919 p. 117

JWs live in a world in which demons and wicked spirits are floating all around. They're twirling their spirit mustaches and cackling as they do dastardly deeds. When I lived in western New York State, the next congregation over from us had Lily Dale, New York in its assigned preaching area. Lily Dale is a tiny hamlet, population 275. It's unique because basically every resident there is a spirit medium. People visit to have their fortunes told. It's been a major center of Spiritualism since its founding in 1879 (coincidentally the same year the *Watchtower* magazine started up).

The interesting thing is the local Dunkirk congregation never enters Lily Dale to preach. JW headquarters has made it literally forbidden territory. I'm not sure there's another off-limits place like that in the entire United States. Evidently, it's considered such a concentrated dose of demonism that it would be too dangerous for the average JW to enter. It's like a black hole with Satan at its core—if you pass the event horizon, you ain't coming back.

Jehovah's Witnesses believe that, fortunately, angels are also all over the place to balance the scales. They have an interesting take on what angels are up to. There are no guardian angels; they won't rescue you or appear to you. But angels are guiding the preaching work.

There are countless anecdotes in the literature of a Witness coming to someone's door just as they were praying to God for guidance *("Bearing Thorough Witness" About God's Kingdom*, p. 59 par. 17); just about to kill themselves (*Yearbook* 2010, p. 49); even a hit man just about to kill his target (*Yearbook* 2002, p. 49). The conclusion? Angelic guidance must be the secret sauce.

One might argue that with millions of JWs putting in billions of hours annually preaching, just by sheer coincidence these types of situations will crop up sometimes. But I was always on the lookout for angelic direction, to see if I felt an urge to go to a certain door.

There is one particular experience all JWs have heard. ("Experiences" are what JWs call anecdotes.) A young JW woman is preaching alone in an apartment building. At one door, a very disreputable-looking guy answers. He's not interested in her message. Upon leaving the building, she is pulled away by police, who are shocked she has survived talking to the man. It turns out he is a serial killer, or has people held hostage, or something. No one visiting his apartment has come out alive. When the police capture him, they ask him why he didn't hurt this lone defenseless woman. "She wasn't alone," he replies. "I saw two huge men with her." Okay, I'm getting tingles (boom, *Scott Pilgrim* reference).

There's a whole subgenre of JW urban legends like that. The broke pioneer who has run out of food, but instead of going to look for a job, decides to put Jehovah first and go preaching. He returns home to find the stoop overflowing with bags of groceries. Or an unexpected check has arrived in the mail. (My parents would sometimes do their own version. They would get a money order for someone and sign it "Pastor Russell," the Witnesses' first president.)

In published articles, JW writers regularly cite the experiences of a purportedly real Witness named Andre (variously written with and without the accent mark). Andre has evidently had a bewildering number of things happen in his life, each of them conveniently just what the article needed to make its point.

And how about Smurfs, the little blue guys created by a Belgian cartoonist in 1958? When my family became Witnesses in the 1980s, the Smurfs were a very popular TV cartoon. Although never mentioned by name in Watchtower literature, they were "known" by American JWs to be demonic. Stories circulated between congregations of Witnesses who had seen Smurf dolls come to life, or had watched Smurfs jump down off Smurf wallpaper and bite children.

ENTERTAINMENT

"Does any of my entertainment involve **spiritism?**

Does it feature such things as vampires, zombies, or the paranormal?

Does it portray magic, spells, or curses as harmless fun?"

- *Watchtower* 04/19, p. 23

Twilight, *Harry Potter*, *World War Z*—they're all off the table for good Witnesses. The organization was nonplussed, to say the least, when in 1974 an active JW (at the time) named Gary Gygax created the game "Dungeons and Dragons."

"Another popular game is called **Dungeons and Dragons.** In this, players assume the roles of monsters, demons, and demigods, as well as of murderers, arsonists, rapists, and torturers. Pleasant company to have in your living room? It often involves players' acting out spiritism and magic. Does that sound healthy to you? It certainly is not".

- *Awake* 07/15/83, p. 28

One of the elders in my congregation was really into music. He'd developed a theory that, since according to 1 John 5:19 the whole earth lay in Satan's power, Satan would grant artists fame and fortune if they honored him by doing at least one work about the occult or supernatural. (I'd never heard of the Charlie Daniels Band back then, but I'd wager this elder just might have.) We came up with lots of examples: "Bad Moon Rising" (Creedence Clearwater Revival), "Highway to Hell" (AC/DC), "Black Magic Woman" (Santana), the *Harry Potter* series (J. K. Rowling), and the *Goosebumps* series (R. L. Stine).

For Witnesses, the main issue isn't people being possessed, and they don't do exorcisms (at least to my knowledge). The trouble with demons is instead almost always to do with a demonized object. They're akin to Portkeys, for *Harry Potter* fans. If you have a thing that's demonized, it becomes a portal allowing the demons into your home. They will disrupt your sleep, move things, rattle doors, and generally terrify you.

Blatantly demonic things like Ouija boards and lucky rabbits' feet obviously need to be destroyed. More specifically, they need to be burned with fire. That's the Bible-approved way to get rid of demonized stuff.

"Indeed, quite a number of those who practiced *magical arts* brought their books together and **burned them up** before everybody.

And they calculated their value and found them worth 50,000 pieces of silver."

- Acts 19:19

When the Scholastic book fair would come around to elementary school, for some reason I always wanted a rabbit's foot keychain which they had for sale. ("Book fair" was a flexible term.) I was jealous of the "worldly" (non-JW) boys who were allowed to buy one. But even non-occult items can carry the demon touch, if previously owned by Spiritualists. Many JWs are wary about buying stuff at garage sales for that reason. When we went to yard sales, first we'd check whether they had a box of books or videos for sale. If they did, we'd look through them to make sure there was no paranormal literature. Only then was it safe to buy a sweater or knick-knack.

A *Watchtower* article from way back in 1966 gave the core tips JWs still abide by today to manage demonic harassment. Here are some tidbits.

"One must be absolutely free of any **relics** of **spiritism,** so as to allow the **demons** no *beachhead."*

"In some few cases the **house** may be the cause of trouble and the best thing to do is **move out...**

Does it have a history of being **haunted?**

Neighbors usually know, though the seller of a house almost always keeps the fact **concealed."**

"Have you accepted any **gifts** from relatives or persons who dabble in spiritism? ...In some *actual cases* it has been a radio, **a sewing machine,** a pair of shoes, jewelry, a 'good luck' charm, **a bathrobe,** a blanket, **a book.** One woman had her bed tipped up at night when she tried to sleep on a **mattress** given her by her Spiritualist mother."

"Actual cases" means these are not theoretical "for-instances." They're real-life situations reliable elders and circuit overseers reported handling in the congregations.

"However, sometimes objects through which demons make contact **resist burning,** indicating **demonic anger** at efforts to destroy them...

Others have reported experiences similar to that of the woman who had much distress at home after **wearing a dress** originally belonging to a *witch.* Learning of the source of trouble, she set out to **burn it.** 'We poured **gasoline** on it, so it would burn quickly; but what amazed us very much was the fact that the dress did not want to burn.'"

Even as a JW kid with no personal experience, I knew the process. You and the elders prayerfully search the house until you find the demonized object(s). You take it to the back yard, get a bonfire going, and put the item in the fire. It will probably refuse to burn. The elders will have to pray around the fire, maybe all night, until it's finally destroyed. At that point, your harassment from demons should gradually fade away in the days and weeks to follow. If not, rinse and repeat.

They leave us with a final pro tip.

ENTERTAINMENT

"When investigating objects, be reasonable, however. Do not burn up *everything* in fearful panic."

- *Watchtower* 12/15/66, pp. 742-743

🌙

The fascination with the power of demons has percolated into the zeitgeist of JW culture so firmly that now when the subject comes up in the literature, the counsel isn't how to get rid of demons. The exasperated writers want JWs to quit spreading the darn tales in the first place.

"Stories about **powerful acts of demons** abound. Such stories are often told with **relish**; people are **fascinated** by them...

Should we share in spreading such stories? No...even if a Christian had some **real encounters** with wicked spirits in the past, he would refrain from **repeatedly** entertaining fellow believers with stories about such things."

- "Keep Yourselves in God's Love"
pp. 194-195, par. 19, 21

What I didn't quite get for a long time is that the Bible is actually filled with magic and wizards. It just uses different labels. The wizards are called prophets; the witches are called prophetesses; the spells and curses are called miracles; the fortune telling is called prophecy. There is an overarching storyline of invisible forces of good and evil united with their respective human allies, battling down through the ages for supremacy.

Let's face it, Moses and Gandalf are pretty much the same character. Aslan the lion is Jesus. Ron Weasly is the Apostle Peter. It cracks me up to think how much effort JWs put into avoiding magic and evil spirits, when the Bible under their arm is the OG fantasy novel. It has ten times as much *everything* as George R. R. Martin has stuffed into his books.

And in the meantime, there's so many great creative works that JWs miss out on. Come on, when I finally saw *The Wizard of Oz* around age thirty-five? It was awesome! And don't get me started on *Harry Potter*.

College

"Vivir con miedo es como vivir a medias."

("A life lived in fear is a life half lived.")

- Strictly Ballroom

The life of a Witness is filled with fear. I know, I know, sweeping statement alert. But it's true, I think. I was constantly scared of doing something which would boot me off the road to eternal life.

Whenever I thought about Jesus' words that "narrow is the gate and cramped the road leading off into life, and few are the ones finding it" (Matthew 7:14), I always pictured it like Frank Capra's film *Lost Horizon*. It was a Shangri-La hidden away in the Himalayas. And a single misstep on the way could plunge me into oblivion. I needed to watch what I said, how I acted, what I wore, and who I was with. That was the key to success. That would get me to paradise in one piece.

But the fear bled into other parts of my life. I was constantly scared about money. I was working a job as a security guard, which didn't pay much. I had another Witness as a roommate to make ends meet. Our rent was $350 per month, split two ways, and it was still tight. Then the factory's security contract was sold to another company. I was petrified the new company might replace me and all my coworkers. It turned out they kept everyone, and the only thing that changed was the uniform. But it made me realize how precarious my living situation was. What skills did I have if that job ever *did* let me go?

A year earlier, my company had offered a one-dollar raise to any guard who finished an EMT-Basic course. The factory wanted more first responders on site. Considering it was about a ten percent bump in pay, I jumped at the opportunity. The classes were once a week on Wednesday nights. At the time, Witnesses were required to attend five hours of meetings each week, divided between Sunday and two weekday evenings (since reduced to one evening). But Wednesday wasn't a meeting night for me, so it would be allowed.

College

I felt uneasy being around so many people who weren't JWs. All of them seemed to know each other from local volunteer fire departments. During class breaks, I sat by myself or walked laps around the parking lot. But I loved learning how to be an EMT. I knew preaching was obviously the best way to help people because then they'd live forever, but this was teaching me you could also help people in a more immediate way. They were bleeding, now they weren't. Their heart was stopped, now it wasn't.

I'd walk my rounds at the plant, reciting the S-A-M-P-L-E mnemonic of what to ask at an incident: Signs and symptoms, Allergies, current Medications, Past medical history, Last meal, and Events leading up to the incident. It was a rare day anything actually happened at the site. Another young guy I worked with was on duty when a man collapsed from a ruptured brain aneurysm. The guard did CPR, but the man was probably dead before he hit the ground. The kid quit that day, and I never saw him again.

I thought about leaving the factory to work on an ambulance, but because of what I'd read in JW literature, I wasn't too sure. I liked reading old issues of the *Awake* magazine. The January 22, 1983 issue had a cover series on paramedics. In it, a JW paramedic described patients he'd had who were high on PCP. One snapped a pair of handcuffs in half, and another needed six guys to hold him down. That didn't sound like anything I wanted to deal with. I was a security guard who tried to avoid confrontation.

I had a Witness friend named Crystal who was a registered nurse. I knew she only worked three days each week, yet could afford her own apartment. That was pretty much all the convincing I needed, and I started getting my prerequisite courses done to enter nursing school at the local community college. There were other pluses—the tuition was cheap, and it was only a two-year degree.

That was important, because unlike almost any other group, JWs highly discourage college education.

"A sister who has been in full-time service for over 15 years says:

'As a baptized Witness, I had read and heard about the **dangers** of pursuing university education, but I dismissed such **warnings**...

Thankfully, once I realized that being **immersed** in higher education was **damaging** my relationship with Jehovah, I knew I had to **stop** and I did...

That time in my life showed me just how **dangerous** it is to ignore the **warnings** given by our Heavenly Father through his organization.

Jehovah knew me better than I knew myself. If **only** I had listened!'"

- *Watchtower* 06/19, p. 6, par. 15-16

The article doesn't mention if she had any trouble covering her student loan payment, which would have kicked in six months after she dropped out. (I'll skip commenting on the clunky dialogue.) Many Christian denominations start Bible colleges. The Latter-day Saints have Brigham Young University. But JWs have always avoided college. It's framed as a hotbed of sex and drinking. Even worse is the emphasis on learning evolution and philosophy. And worst of all, time in college is time you're unable to use for the Watchtower organization. Besides, isn't the world about to end anyway?

"If you are a young person,
   you also need to face the fact that
   you
   will

never

   grow
   old
   in this present system of things...

If you are in high school and thinking about a college education, it means at least four, perhaps even six or eight more years to graduate into a specialized career. But where will this system of things be by that time? It will be well on the way toward its finish, if not actually

                            gone!"

                - *Awake* 05/22/**1969**, p. 15

Just to emphasize, published in ***1969***. My dad was college age in 1969. He worked an entire career, and retired a couple of years ago. But using JW-land reasoning, the article wasn't wrong. It just means we're fifty years *closer* to Armageddon. It would be even *more* nutty to go to college now.

In my congregation there was an older man named Clarence. He had been involved in the ground floor of computers in the mid-twentieth century. However, he gave it up to be a pioneer for most of his life. He didn't regret his decision, but he sometimes spoke a bit wistfully of what might have been, as he wore his neat but threadbare suits, tried to stretch his Social Security check to last all month, and drove his car that was on its last legs.

The organization recommends various alternatives to university: technical or vocational schools, or, worst-case scenario, an associate degree.

"Many such institutions offer *short* courses in

    office skills,

    auto repair,

    computer repair,

    plumbing,

    hairdressing,

    and a host of other trades.

Are these desirable jobs?

Certainly!"

- *Watchtower* 10/01/05, p. 31

Obviously, trades such as electrician or plumber can be good fields to get into, from the standpoint of both job security and salary. However, it is a bit disingenuous when one considers a 2016 letter sent from headquarters to all congregations. The letter asked congregation elders to identify local JWs with college education who could be used by the branch office on projects. And they weren't looking for hairdressers or car mechanics.

"There is an **urgent** need to locate... **skilled** brothers... to assist with large-scale theocratic construction projects, computer-related projects, audio/video projects, and the increasing translation work...

Please note that we are **not** encouraging anyone to pursue higher education or university degrees to obtain certain skills."

— "Skills Questionnaire Instructions"
A-2i-E US 02/16
(Bold theirs)

If a young Witness goes to college, they typically go on the naughty list as "spiritually weak." They won't face a judicial committee (see glossary or Chap. 10), but they and their parents are going to get a lot of judgmental judginess from congregation members. If her father is an elder, he may be voluntold to "step down"—to resign his position as an elder.

However, as soon as she graduates, she will often be recruited by the organization as a valuable asset. She may be called to Bethel headquarters to work. The rare physician or dentist who later becomes a JW after his schooling is eagerly headhunted by the organization to provide services at Bethel. A house is given to him and his family, and all their expenses are paid for as long as he or she can be persuaded to stay.

If the pool of available college-educated workers willing to work for free is too small, headquarters will send Bethelites to college, paying their tuition with the donations from JWs. (Funding university education for Bethelites probably isn't the first thing which comes to mind when Witnesses think about how their donations will be used.) In recent years, the focus has been on creating attorneys. Lots of attorneys. Lawyers are essential for defending child sexual abuse cases domestically, and fighting restrictions on organization activity abroad. And a Bethel lawyer is a lawyer with no billable hours. Covering their law school tuition is a small investment which pays dividends for decades.

My two-year degree was not ideal from a JW standpoint, but as long as I kept up my congregation responsibilities, it could work. In essence, nobody should be able to tell I was in college. I couldn't have a drop-off in hours spent preaching or meeting attendance, and I better not get any more independent in my dress or attitude. I pulled it off like a champ.

In my classes, I learned about "the nursing process," known by the catchy acronym ANDPIE. It stands for Assessment, Nursing Diagnosis, Planning, Intervention, and Evaluation. It describes the basic way most fields of human endeavor do things: collect information, create a plan, execute the plan, and evaluate how it went.

The concept fascinated me, because as a JW, I didn't use that process at all. Instead, I read the information provided for me, agreed with the plan given to me, did whatever it said, and didn't evaluate anything. To do anything else was to display an independent spirit.

"Strive in all aspects of life to show that you **reject an independent spirit** and that you **accept Jehovah's authority.**"

- *Watchtower* 06/15/08, p. 22, par. 18

"All of us must be ready to **obey** *any* instructions we may receive, whether these appear sound from a strategic or human standpoint *or not.*"

- *Watchtower* 11/15/13, p. 20, par. 17

This gets at the core of why the JW organization discourages college—it teaches you how to think. The subject matter isn't the issue, even something like evolutionary biology. The fundamental problem is that you learn how to take a topic, research it objectively, take action based on your conclusions, and then reevaluate. Critical thinking is death to groups like Jehovah's Witnesses. And sure enough, many young JWs who go off to college drift away permanently from the faith.

The constant instruction against higher education has worked, more or less. A 2014 Pew Research study ranked thirty major religious groups by education level. Jehovah's Witnesses came in third from the bottom, with only twelve percent of JW respondents reporting a college degree. However, an unintended side effect has been the lack of donations coming in. A high school diploma isn't what it was fifty years ago in the job market. Congregations full of window washers and office cleaners aren't able to contribute like they would with higher-paying jobs. The organization has had to cut back in response. Twenty percent of global Bethel staff were let go in 2016.

"Stephen Lett of the Governing Body further explained...

> 'many long-standing Bethel routines and services are being reduced or eliminated.
>
> This will result in fewer members of the Bethel family being required.'
>
> Hence, since September 2015, some
>
> **5,500**
>
> members of the Bethel family have returned to the field."

- Yearbook 2017, p. 10

The organization has also had to dial back the reading level at which it writes the literature. In 2011, they needed to begin releasing the *Watchtower* magazine in both a standard version and a simplified edition for lower reading skills. In 2019, they were able to discontinue the simplified edition. Why? As announced at the 2017 Annual Meeting, the reading grade level of the regular edition had been reduced enough to make a separate edition superfluous. (The Annual Meeting is a one-day conference at world headquarters. The organization uses it to announce new insights. It's kind of like an Apple product launch, if Apple made iBibles.)

In 2013 they released a revised edition of the Bible that Jehovah's Witnesses produce, the *New World Translation of the Holy Scriptures*. It, too, decreased the reading level required. Editors cut the word count by ten percent. JWs typically study two books about Witness teachings with a potential convert to get them to the point of baptism and beyond. Each has been replaced with a simpler edition in recent years. An analysis of these books using the standard Flesch-Kincaid readability tests is illuminating. The JW book used during the 1970s, *The Truth That Leads to Eternal Life*, was written at an eleventh-grade reading level. The current study book, *What Can the Bible Teach Us?*, was released in 2015. It is written at a level appropriate for ten-year-old children.

I sometimes wonder if the organization ever regrets its long-time stance against college education. Is it better to have a larger number of poor—and poorly educated—members, or fewer—but wealthier—ones? Does the Governing Body ever gaze out of its boardroom windows, ruefully thinking of what might have been, if only the early JW leaders had modeled the Latter-day Saints' technique of advocating both higher education and tithing?

College

As my own classes wrapped up, I began to worry about graduation. I was proud of what I'd accomplished. However, the Bible clearly indicates pride is a sin. Pride over getting a college degree was even worse. I'd homeschooled in high school, so I never experienced walking across a stage to shake the principal's hand as my name was announced. I just sent in the last test, and that was that. My diploma had come in the mail, a piece of paper folded in half inside a flimsy blue plastic sleeve. (I liked to say I graduated at the top of my class and also at the bottom.)

Maybe I should have been pleased that now I could have a graduation, to make up for missing my high school one. But I wasn't. For JWs, the world is divided into two camps: Satan's and Jehovah's. If you aren't in one, you're in the other. No fence-sitters are allowed. I recall one speaker explaining that Satan owned the fence. Another described the fence as a big razor blade, impossible to straddle. All my graduation would do is show onlookers I'd slid a bit more toward Satan's side. It was an occasion for shame. I ignored the announcements about getting your cap and gown.

But then I learned nursing school offered a third road which did straddle the line just a bit between God and Satan's world. As in most nursing programs, there would be a pinning ceremony at the end of the semester. A remnant of traditions a century old, students come to the stage one by one, and a relative or teacher fastens a small pin chosen by the class to their lapel. The pin aptly symbolizes that they are ready to go out into the world and poke patients with things.

I decided the pinning ceremony would be acceptable. I invited my parents and sister to attend, and I asked my mom to do the pinning. It felt right, just the correct amount of pride without straying over the line. School ended, and a few weeks later I stopped in to pick up my diploma from the registrar's office.

I began working in a local hospital where I'd done clinical rotations. I was still scared of many things, but at least living on the street because I couldn't pay my rent wasn't one of them. The little confidence boost from successfully completing something like a college degree bled into everything else. I had proved my brain wasn't completely terrible. It worked for evaluating someone's blood pressure, and for figuring out how to keep a confused patient in bed. There was just one thing I hadn't reckoned with. Brains are feisty little critters. My brain had gotten a taste for assessment, and now it wanted to assess everything. Peanut butter. Car tires. Driving routes.

And eventually, my entire worldview.

Watchtower, Inc.

I'M LISTENING TO THE JAKE BRAKES OF THE TRUCKS GOING BY outside. It's all good. I mean, who needs sleep anyway? Hmm, so who exactly was Jake to get brakes named after him? *googles* Ah, it was a guy named Clessie Cummins. It all makes perfect sense.

I actually used to work at a Cummins plant back in the day. Sometimes on the weekend I would go up on the enormous flat roof, which covered 1,000,000 ft^2. I'd climb a maintenance ladder and pretend I was standing at the bow of a ship. The wind was in my hair and peanut M&Ms were in my pocket. It was just like the *Titanic* poster. That I knew for sure. But was it just like the actual movie? That was trickier, considering I'd never seen it. I was a good JW, which meant Kate Winslet's breasts were, tragically, a deal breaker.

I had a lot of free time at that job. I'd often ruminate about Jehovah's Witnesses, among other things. Sometimes there were things which didn't quite make sense. Like, why did we have to turn in a report at the end of each month of how much we preached? I've never really seen anything like that in the Bible. I'm pretty sure no

Catholics or Baptists do that. I now know Latter-day Saints do, during their two-year missionary tour.

Be that as it may (I'll gratuitously use that phrase here because it's awesome), reporting time makes more sense when you picture Jehovah's Witnesses as a sort of multi-level marketing, book-publishing corporation. JWs have always been proud of their publishing heritage. I imagine that was part of the reason it was decided early on to call everyone approved to preach door to door a "publisher," instead of perhaps the more expected term of "teacher" or "preacher."

The founder, Charles Russell, named it the "Zion's Watch Tower Tract Society." Emphasis on "Tract Society." Right from the start, printing and distributing tracts (the old-timey word for pamphlets), magazines, and books was really important to him, and that's what most of the money went towards. Eventually, the Society started buying their own printing presses and had volunteers run them (in exchange for room and board), which dropped the cost substantially.

In the early days, the Society had sales reps called "colporteurs." It's an archaic word. A colporteur by definition is somebody who sells religious books door to door. They could support themselves (just barely) selling Watch Tower literature house to house as a job, because back in the day the Society paid a commission on sales of books and magazine subscriptions. It was a straight commission job though, no base salary. Colporteurs pretty much lived hand to mouth. They had to cover a lot of territory to make enough to survive.

"Brother Holland explained:
   'Sometimes I went without breakfast;
   sometimes I had a few slices of bread
   without butter...
   My shoes were wearing out
   and my feet would get wet,' he recalls.

'Then one sunny day
as I was walking along a country road,
it got very warm,
and the tar on the road began to melt.

The tar filled the holes
      in the soles
         of my shoes.

   So I got my shoes "mended."'
   And that was without cost!"

- Yearbook 1988, p. 86

I need to point out that Brother Holland here, and all the other colporteurs cited in articles, talk about how happy they were doing God's work. That's how it is with just about anything to do with the Watchtower organization. You can see it as a selfless institution to which members are glad to willingly donate their time and money. Or you can look at it as a calculating entity which plays the religion and guilt card to prosper at the expense of the rank and file. The truth is probably somewhere in the middle.

I will say the organization always seems to come out ahead in whatever directives it gives its adherents. A recent example was in 2014. A letter from headquarters dated March 29 was read out forgiving all Kingdom Hall mortgages. (JW meeting houses are called "Kingdom Halls" instead of "churches.") As a rule, all congregations approved by the Watchtower organization to build a new Kingdom Hall get their mortgage from the organization itself, instead of from a bank. So it seemed, for all intents and purposes, to be a loving change. But only one page of a four-page letter was read to the congregation.

The remainder contained detailed instructions to the elders. It explained that in place of the mortgage, congregations were to continue paying at least the same amount, except now with no end date. It was, in effect, a mortgage which would last until the cows come home. Some congregations had paid off their mortgages years ago. They were advised to take a survey of how much everyone could contribute, and start paying that amount each month to the organization. That's the way these things always seem to go in the JW religion. And how much you know about the true reasons for a change depends on the level you're at. Or who you know that's a muckety-muck.

WATCHTOWER, INC.

"This postscript should **not** be read to the congregation, and this letter should **not** be posted on the information board."

- "Letter to all Congregations"
03/29/14 (Bold theirs)

In 1931, the title "colporteur" was changed to "pioneer." The Society got on a bit of a military-themed kick for a while. I don't know, maybe they liked the Salvation Army setup. A pioneer was a military combat engineer who helped pave the way as an army advanced. The United States military had multiple Pioneer Battalions over the decades. The name change from colporteur also helped rebrand them as more than just book salesmen.

Actually, that same year they rebranded the whole religion, changing the name from the rather generic "Bible Students" to "Jehovah's Witnesses." I was always very particular about the grammar. If someone said, "You're a Jehovah Witness," no apostrophe, that bugged me. The only correct way was to say, "I'm *one of* Jehovah's Witnesses," i.e., you are a witness for this person Jehovah. Unfortunately, it's not a witness like "eyewitness." We're clearly in a millennia-long lull where Jehovah God is declining to do any miracles and show himself.

I remember when I first read Douglas Adams' *Hitchhiker's Guide to the Galaxy* series. My friend Brian turned me on to the books. Brian was a geek, in the cool modern sense. He was married to Holly, an attractive, funny woman, and hence had pulled off the ultimate geek hat trick. (Holly's sense of humor was wickedly good. One time she was visiting friends when some local JWs happened to be canvassing the street. Using her years of experience as a pioneer, she began raising objection after objection to every point they tried to make. Only when they were thoroughly drenched with flop-sweat did she give up the gig and admit she was a JW too.)

One particular day, news spread like wildfire through the congregation: Brian had gone to see a *Lord of the Rings* movie. JWs are very proud to say they don't have to publish lists of movies or albums that are forbidden. They explain it's because their Bible-trained consciences are so finely honed. But probably more influential is a palpable social pressure exerted by the congregation of what is and isn't acceptable. Tolkien was bad, because magic and wizards. So Brian was cool and edgy to me. I'd never have dared to go see those movies.

But anyway, Hitchhiker's Guide. In *So Long and Thanks for All the Fish,* Adams writes that God's Final Message to His Creation is written in thirty-foot-high letters of fire on top of the Quentulus Quazgar Mountains in the land of Sevorbeupstry on the planet Preliumtarn, third out from the sun Zarss, in Galactic Sector QQ7 Active J Gamma. And I got to wondering, hey, why *couldn't* Jehovah do that, just to clear up everything?

Of course, for JWs (and, I imagine, most faiths) there is a complex reasoning laid out as to why we would actually be worse Christians if everything was clear and proven. They say cultivating a strong faith is what makes a really first-rate JW. Still, I always thought it would make the preaching work much easier if, while at the door, you could just point up at the giant letters of fire on the moon which said JWs were the one true religion.

So if it's not "Jehovah's Eyewitnesses," how exactly was I a witness? It was more like being called to testify in a court case and attest to someone's character. It was my job to explain why, even though Jehovah is all-powerful and all-seeing, he is not actually a jerk for allowing the Holocaust and any number of other atrocities. Also, it's taken from the Bible.

"'You are my witnesses,' declares Jehovah, 'Yes, my servant whom I have chosen.'"

- Isaiah 43:10

The name change was a nifty brainwave which helped lend some gravitas to a religion barely fifty years old at the time. Now they could say the Bible kinda sorta prophesied they'd come along. Other terms also changed at the time. Continuing the military theme, congregations became "companies." Elders became "company servants." Seventy-eight divisions comprised of JW volunteers were formed in the United States. If a town was considered to be giving local Witnesses a hassle about preaching, a "divisional campaign" was organized. The nearest division swarmed the town with hundreds of Witnesses all preaching on a single morning, overwhelming local police.

"The
New Jersey
battle front,
being the
hottest,
frequently required
the large
New York
and
New Jersey
divisions
of
200 car units each
(comprising
a thousand 'locusts'
each)
to
go into action
alternately,
depending upon
the weekly arrests."

- *Watchtower* 07/15/55, p. 427

By this time, the country was divided up into sales territories. To this day, each congregation has an assigned territory, managed by the local group of elders. Each congregation territory is subdivided into dozens of smaller territories. JWs can check them out like a library book, so that the entire area is covered systematically. City congregations might knock out their territory every few weeks. Rural ones might take a year or more.

About twenty congregations are grouped into a circuit, managed by a circuit overseer. For many decades, a group of circuits formed a district, managed by a district overseer. The district overseer layer of management was eliminated in 2014. Most district overseers were demoted back down to circuit overseers, unless they had already hit the circuit overseer age cutoff of seventy years old, in which case their traveling overseer career abruptly ended.

As mentioned, one rather peculiar aspect of JWs is the requirement to turn in a report at the end of each month. Reported first and foremost is the number of hours spent preaching door to door (or other current JW-approved preaching style, such as standing by a literature cart on the street). The report historically included how many books and magazines were given out to people ("placed," in JW parlance). Nowadays, you can also list things such as how many times you played a video to individuals. The amount of literature was always important, although not as important as the hours. Say you spent twenty hours preaching, but only gave out two magazines the whole time. That meant you were slacking. You needed to step up your game, son!

To explain this rule about filing a report each month, JWs are quick to point out a couple of spots in the Bible where Jesus' disciples shared their preaching results with each other. However, I don't think they were tallying up how many hours they spent, or how many times they opened a scroll. In my own experience, it creates an environment in which it's impossible not to feel that the more hours you put in, the more spiritual you are. Of course, JWs are careful to say salvation cannot be earned, per se. On the other hand, a verse frequently trotted out is "faith without works is dead" (James 2:26), with "works" explained as the door-to-door preaching.

Advancement as a JW is closely tied to how many hours you put in each month. While there is no official quota, the minimum for the average JW publisher is expected to be the national average, usually about ten hours per month. You can go preaching any time you like, but the most popular time for Witnesses is Saturday mornings. JW kids don't get to eat Chocolate Frosted Sugar Bombs while watching Saturday cartoons. Instead, I'd wake up and look over the current magazines, formulate my sales pitch—my "presentation"—and then rehearse it, with Susannah or my dad role-playing the person answering the door.

An auxiliary pioneer is someone who picks one month to do fifty hours. A regular auxiliary pioneer does fifty hours each month indefinitely. A regular pioneer does seventy hours each month indefinitely. (The hour requirement has by necessity been lowered over the years. Since college education is discouraged, pioneers need to work a lot of hours at menial jobs to make ends meet. And numerically, it's better to have five pioneers doing seventy hours per month than two doing one hundred hours.) Special pioneers (who are appointed by the organization) do 130 hours each month, and they receive a stipend. Missionaries are similar to special pioneers, but generally are stationed in a foreign country.

Each level carries increasing esteem among JWs. As an example, if you're a missionary coming back home for a visit (they're allowed home once every three years), you can expect to be asked to give the

Sunday talk at the hall, present a slide show about your assignment, be interviewed at a regional convention if one is going on, and anything else that can be stuffed in while you're there.

On the other end, drop below the national average, say down to five hours in a month, and you're noted to be a "low hour publisher." If a month passes with zero preaching, you're "irregular." Break out the Metamucil. If six months go by, you're officially "inactive." The congregation elders note each of these with increasing alarm. While not a formal JW system, many elders have come up with a method of rating publishers using a green, yellow, or red color to assess their standing.

The circuit overseer visits each congregation every six months. He spends a week with them to assess what they're doing well, and what they need to improve. He will particularly request that two sets of records be available for review when he arrives in town Tuesday afternoon. One is the dollar amount of donations being sent to headquarters, and the second is the publisher activity individually and as a whole. Say the average hours are dropping, or the number of irregular publishers is increasing. The congregation can expect very pointed talks about being zealous and not letting their love cool off. His meetings with the local elders will be even more blunt.

I'm not sure any other religion focuses as intensely on the numbers as JWs do. But if you think for a moment about, not a religion, but a company that sells products, data is everything. The organizational structure of sales territories and layers of middle management all starts to make perfect sense.

Until 1990, JWs could very much be described as a religious bookseller. They printed a thirty-two-page magazine each week, alternating between the *Watchtower* and *Awake*. Every publisher had a standing order for multiple copies—one for personal study and some more to resell while preaching. Depending what year you're looking at, that was ten or twenty million guaranteed sales of every issue. (The circulation is up around forty million nowadays.)

The magazines cost a quarter apiece when I was growing up. It's safe to say there was a comfortable profit margin built into this figure. Although JWs are categorized as a nonprofit organization, that isn't to say they priced the magazines at their cost. Instead, the entire organization was funded largely on the back of the literature sales. In fact, regular pioneers (who often might have a standing order for dozens of copies to use in their door-to-door work) could purchase the magazines at a discount, and then sell them in the community at face value. (The sales commissions are long gone.) The profit wasn't much, but it would probably cover their coffee break if they hustled.

The key piece of the puzzle is understanding that the Watchtower Society's customers were not the public. Their customers were the congregation members. If you didn't use all the issues you bought, that was too bad, but you couldn't return them for a refund. The Society's money was made.

(My congregation had to make announcements once in a while reminding everyone that dumping a pile of ten or twenty old magazines in a bus stop or laundromat to boost your numbers wasn't cool. Two at a time was okay though. Sometimes on winter days we would go to the local hospital and hit every single waiting room. We weren't there to talk to people. We wanted to leave old magazines in each one, if no one else had beaten us to it.)

Each year at the annual summer conventions, headquarters typically announced a new book they had for sale. Again, every single JW would eagerly buy at least one copy. They usually cost about one dollar. There were so many publications you could purchase, from four-page pamphlets (a penny) up to deluxe leather Bibles with shiny gold edging on each page (seven dollars). The system worked incredibly well—until, that is, Jimmy Swaggart and the state of California had to go and gum up the works.

In 1990 an extraordinary letter was read to the congregation. I was eleven, and distinctly remember how much talk there was when it was read out that JWs would no longer charge money for any of their literature. Instead, we would ask for a voluntary donation from the householder. I recall we were trying to figure out how that made any financial sense. At the same time, we were relieved that the awkward part of our sales pitch where we asked for fifty cents for the two magazines was gone.

Bill was one of the elders in our congregation. Before getting married, he'd spent many years working at Bethel headquarters. He quietly explained to some of us that his old Bethel buddies had given him the inside scoop. (I was undoubtedly lurking in the periphery as he talked to my parents; I usually preferred hanging around the adults.) Bill said the real reason for the change was not to simplify the preaching work, as the letter had stated. Rather, it was because otherwise the Society would have had to start paying taxes. And Bill was exactly right.

"Jimmy Swaggart Ministries" is the publishing arm of the eponymous televangelist. In 1980 it was notified by the state of California that although religions themselves aren't taxed, it should have been remitting sales tax on religious literature it sold in the state. Swaggart challenged this in court, and the case slowly wended its way to the U.S. Supreme Court. The Watchtower Society began watching the case with great interest.

They realized that if Swaggart lost, they too could be on the hook for a sizable amount of back taxes. And the idea of each congregation publisher collecting sales tax, and filing a quarterly tax return as an independent contractor, didn't sound real hot to the Society. It would make the religion's core operation since the 1880s—selling magazines and books—a bit too transparent to rank-and-file JWs. In public, they excoriated Jimmy Swaggart for his sex scandal and his lavish lifestyle.

"*Newsweek* reported that George Jernigan, a former executive of Swaggart's, claimed that Swaggart 'raised $20 million for a children's fund but spent **less than 10 percent of it** on the program.'

... collected for one purpose, then used for another, for personal enrichment-

that's embezzlement.

The Pharisees were **money lovers.**

Judas sold out Christ for money.

Many religious leaders today walk in their footsteps rather than those of Jesus."

- *Awake* 03/22/88, p. 7

But simultaneously they took the surprising step of quietly filing an *amicus curiae*—"friend of the court"—brief with the Supreme Court in 1989 supporting Jimmy Swaggart. Evidently desperate times call for desperate measures. The Supreme Court ruled against Swaggart in 1990. A few weeks later was when I heard that surprising letter read out.

Incidentally, by 1992 it was back to business as usual castigating Swaggart in the pages of *Awake*.

"Misconduct by religious leaders is catching the public eye today as never before.

Protestants have been embarrassed by the scandalous conduct of TV ministers.

After [Swaggart] was recently caught with a prostitute for the second time in three years,

he informed his followers that God told him that his behavior was nobody's business but his own."

- *Awake* 05/08/92, p. 26

It's clear that over the next few years, the Society's income took a sizable dive. Voluntary donations were simply not matching what had been coming in before, despite innumerable articles explaining how to ask for donations, and countless demonstrations at the meetings of how to do it.

I can say that personally, asking for a donation turned out to be even more uncomfortable than saying the magazines cost a quarter. Who would have guessed that begging for money doesn't come naturally? Like many Witnesses, I often ended up just never mentioning it. It felt strange to be in a pleasant conversation about the Bible with the rare person who was actually interested, and then have to wedge in that this was part of a worldwide work supported by voluntary donations. I'd stop talking in hopes the householder would crack first and give me some change to fill the awkward silence.

WATCHTOWER, INC.

"We also make friends with Jehovah and Jesus

by using our financial resources

to support the work that they are directing."

- *Watchtower* April 2020 p. 24, par. 13

I worked in the literature department in my congregation, as well as the food department at conventions. Each was a disaster after switching to voluntary donations. In the literature department, people who previously couldn't afford them were now ordering leather-bound Bibles and large hardcover reference books like they were going out of style. (Which they did, eventually. Pretty much everything hardcover long ago switched to paperback.)

In 1994 the Society began making a Bible reference computer program on CD-ROM, called "Watchtower Library." Although created and produced by volunteers, announcements to the congregation asked members to consider what *commercial* encyclopedia programs cost, and donate appropriately.

"With that in mind, many publishers estimate what these items might cost if **commercially produced,** and then they *contribute accordingly.* For example, a deluxe, gold-edged Bible can easily cost **$20 or more,** a reference book may be **$40 and up,** a full-color wall calendar may sell for **at least $5,** an encyclopedia on CD-ROM costs from **$50 to $100 or higher,** music compact discs commonly cost **close to $20,** and some videos are often sold for **much more.**"

- *Our Kingdom Ministry* 11/96, p. 3

"Fifty to one hundred dollars or higher" was an astounding sum for many Witnesses. No doubt the organization was trying to subsidize the loss of donations for other products.

The food department had similar problems. Almost since the beginning, the Society sold food at their annual summer conventions, prepared each day by volunteers like my family. Let me tell you, you never ordered roast beef after making a thousand sandwiches from that greasy, stringy meat at 6:00 am. (On the other hand, there was nothing better than going in the refrigerated reefer truck and getting a slushy, half-frozen orange juice.)

The organization had long used an unusual system of tickets to buy food. Each family would use cash to buy however many sheets of tickets they thought would be needed. Then they would pay for each food item with the specified number of tickets. For a few chaotic years after the Supreme Court decision, the Society tried to continue serving food on a donation basis.

It was bad. Kids would run up and grab three cheese danishes and a Shasta pop. Then they'd take off without a glance at the donation box next to the counter. Food service was swiftly discontinued. It was framed as a nice way for all the volunteers to have more time to visit with friends. The direction now is to bring a bag lunch.

It's created a side headache for the organization, because management at convention centers watch as JWs that are a bit rebellious (or just too frazzled to pack a lunch) pour out to area restaurants at lunchtime. They get mad they can't have their concession stands open during conventions, something JW leadership has always resisted. I guess hot dogs and nachos are not "food at the proper time."

However, the closed concessions create some opportunities. My friend Katie related, between giggles, watching two young men working as convention attendants. (An attendant is sort of like a security guard, there to make sure everything is orderly. You get a nifty "Attendant" badge to wear.) Having stationed themselves in front of a hot dog stand, the two watched as girls walked by during the intermissions. Depending on their verdict, they would shift slightly, so that either the word "hot" or "dog" was displayed.

In the years since 1990, the amount of printed literature has been dramatically downsized to match the reduced income. Without a dependable cash flow from each new issue, there was no point in publishing so prolifically. The past output—128 pages of magazines per month—has been slashed by two-thirds, down to a monthly average of 40 pages.

(One might think that if each day brings us closer to Armageddon, the urgency of the times demands the amount of "spiritual food" provided should be increasing, not on the decline. But the organization has evidently not quite seen it that way.)

Giving out magazines and books to the public has been de-emphasized. Instead, JWs play short videos directing people to the JW website. It's an interesting callback to the early days of the Watch Tower Society. In the 1930s, Witnesses would lug around portable phonographs and play records of Watch Tower sermons on the doorstep. (There was also a sound car era, when JWs would drive around town blaring a recorded discourse from loudspeakers mounted on a truck. Thankfully, that hasn't made a comeback just yet.)

In a providential twist, the rise of the Internet coincided with the decreased donations. Witnesses are encouraged to use digital versions of publications instead of physical copies. If a new publication is released, there is a download link provided, instead of cartons of books trucked into each convention. For most of my JW life, a Witness using an e-reader or tablet at the Kingdom Hall would have been rebuked. Now, the meetings are awash in iPads running the official JW-produced app. As in many religions, large flat screens have sprung up in each hall to play JW-produced videos.

"Then there are the preachers
peddling
pop psychology,
the **goody-goody** palaverers

that dole out
the smooth things
to tickle ears
unreceptive to
unvarnished
Bible truth.
Not the
wheat
but the
chaff
is what they feed their flocks."

- Awake 03/22/88, p. 8

Witnesses always maintained that modern churches' slick TV productions and catchy songs were spiritual junk food when compared to their own sober, meaty presentation of Bible truths. In a neighboring congregation to mine, one Witness was quite a good organist. He would play to accompany the singing at meetings. However, eventually he wasn't allowed to play anymore. The higher-ups said it was a bit too jazzy. They switched instead to the more staid prerecorded piano music distributed by the organization.

If Ted were still alive today, he'd probably laugh to see the current setup. The organization now makes its own original music videos, each in a different style, from country to Broadway to smooth R&B. They have built their own TV studios, and are constantly releasing new shows to their website and on streaming devices. They have a children's cartoon series. In 2019, they announced plans to build a large facility in Ramapo, New York dedicated to film and video production. Staffed by a thousand people, it will rival the size of the entire world headquarters complex in Warwick.

The religion has become in some ways a victim of its own success. All those missionaries assigned to impoverished countries in Africa and South America used their 130+ hours each month well. The largest growth in new converts is found in these developing lands. In contrast, most countries in Europe and North America have little or no annual growth. The trouble is many of the new Witnesses have very little materially. They have zeal, but no donations to give. The Internet availability in these countries is often lacking, meaning more printed books and magazines are required.

It will be interesting to see how the organization handles this conundrum in coming years. No doubt things will continue to move online more and more to save money. A gradually increasing percentage of congregation meeting time consists of playing videos. In the past, a substantial portion of each week's meetings was dedicated to a public speaking course. That has been scaled back significantly. Will a time come when local Witnesses do none of their own speaking, and simply tune in to a weekly broadcast from headquarters? And if that were the case, would there even be a need for each town to have a physical hall in which to meet?

As the Magic 8 Ball says, "Cannot predict now." However, the organization has indeed been busy in recent years selling off a considerable number of its meeting houses. It makes sense, because many congregations (particularly the English-language ones) have shrinking attendance. The sales also provide a needed infusion of cash. Constructed with volunteer labor, there is a nice profit to be made selling Kingdom Hall properties. Local congregations keep only a minimum of cash on hand, and all surplus funds are transferred to headquarters. That includes money from Kingdom Hall sales. Indeed, the small number of new halls now being built use a distinctly commercial style created by JW headquarters architects. The design lends itself to being converted directly to a Starbucks or a Verizon store when they're flipped in a few years.

In the days of Watch Tower Society founder Charles Russell, the Bible Students met together as small groups in homes to discuss the Bible, using Russell's books. President Dwight D. Eisenhower's childhood home was one of these. His mother, and for a number of years his father, were Bible Students. Like many adherents, the Eisenhowers had a ten-foot-by-six-foot wall chart hanging in their living room (Holmes, 2012). On it, Russell had diagrammed how the length of passages in the Egyptian pyramids confirmed Bible prophecy. Will things eventually come full circle, so that Jehovah's

Witnesses again meet in small groups in homes, watching the latest JW broadcast?

Organization videos in recent years have depicted their idea of the time just before Armageddon. In these productions, small groups huddle together, hidden Anne Frank-style in attics or basements while heavily armed military squads search for them. According to JW theology, governments will outlaw all religion. Eventually, only Jehovah's Witnesses will remain standing. Satan/the governments (the two are basically one and the same for JWs) will make a final push to wipe out the Witnesses.

In 2018, the organization published the book *Pure Worship of Jehovah—Restored at Last!* An illustration in the book showed generals and other world leaders tensely meeting in a Situation Room. Crumpled *Watchtower* magazines are strewn across the table. A wall of monitors is tuned to the JW Broadcasting channel on one screen, and a live feed of the Bethel headquarters complex on another.

A memorable movie played at 2018 conventions portrayed a small group of JWs standing defenseless in a field. Scores of black-clad soldiers armed with automatic rifles swarm toward them. At the last second, the heavens open up to reveal Jesus Christ astride a gleaming white stallion, golden bow in hand. A myriad of angels follow behind him. The music swells to a mighty crescendo as God steps in to rescue his people and strike down their enemies.

Back in 1999, there was a lot of hype that the Y2K computer bug would bring civilization to a screeching halt. I have to admit I put a few dozen jugs of water in our basement. Just in case, you know. My parents rolled their eyes and shook their heads. Stockpiling supplies was for crazy survivalists who didn't have Jehovah on their side. However, the years since then have seen the organization markedly ramp up the emphasis on preparedness.

On the unofficial Witness forum JWTalk.net, a number of threads discuss what to pack in a "go bag." In one post, a forum moderator writes, "I hope this is helpful, besides the cash that I have at home and in my kits, I also have emergency funds at several different major banks so in case one bank system fails I can use another one" (Bro Richard, 2017).

"Be Prepared!"
— *Awake* 02/07, p. 17

"Also, some families have prepared **'go-bags'** with such items as the following:..."
— *Awake* 2017, No. 5, p. 6

"Are **You** Equipped To **Flee?**"
— *Awake* 09/07, p. 7

Considering this worldview, it's not hard to imagine most JWs being unfazed if all Kingdom Halls are sold off, and their activity shrinks to small meetings in homes. It would simply fit in with their understanding of future events. Instead of signaling a dying organization, it would be a happy sign that world events are progressing as per Bible prophecy. Paradise surely must be just around the corner.

By the way, that's a little secret the JW organization has stumbled on. If bad things happen in the world, it's a sign that we're in "the last days," and deliverance is near. If bad things happen to the JW organization, it confirms they're the true religion, because Jesus said his followers would be persecuted. And if good things happen to JWs, it's a sign of Jehovah God's blessing. Literally anything that happens is a good sign in some way. It helps explain how Witnesses are so resilient as a group, and why it is so difficult to introduce any possibility that JWs might not be the one true religion.

Working as an ICU nurse, I would often see families of grievously injured patients. Some would be so sure of a positive outcome. They would excitedly point out a random eye twitch or hand squeeze as a sign their loved one would wake up. That, despite such traumatic injuries we'd sometimes have to arrange towels to hide the brain matter leaking out of their battered head.

That blazing hope can serve families well, sometimes. But sometimes, it becomes an obstacle to considering other possibilities. There is a window of time in which the death of a person who is irreversibly injured can create life for several others, through organ donation. Down the road, families take great pride and satisfaction that some good came out of their tragedy. But whether they can shift their thinking so radically, to think of it not as giving up and pulling the plug, but as saying goodbye with dignity and love, and giving life to the recipients—that is the question. It's a difficult leap to make. Some families are ultimately unable to do it. But many do, and derive a bittersweet happiness. It is the complete opposite of the outcome they were hoping for, and yet there is a goodness at its core.

I sometimes feel that is what Jehovah's Witnesses are like. They latch on to any little sign confirming their beliefs. In some ways JWs are very positive people. They have an unwavering hope which says that ultimately, things will work out well. They believe beyond a doubt that soon they will be living forever in a paradise on earth.

However, it makes it an almost insurmountable task to consider the possibility of ever not being a JW. Growing beyond the organization might mean saying goodbye to hopes, dreams, and people they love with their whole heart, soul, mind, and strength. It is the complete opposite of the outcome they were hoping for. Yet, again, there is goodness encapsulated deep within such a decision. To go all *Sound of Music*, when God closes a door, somewhere he opens a window. Changing one's beliefs about a faith tradition may close a door through which a wistful hope of eternal life in a Garden of Eden beckoned. But it opens others leading to new friends, lovers, education, and experiences which otherwise would never have existed.

"It is an essential truth about life that
every time you make a decision,
you also experience
a **loss** of some alternative...

When you buy a
chocolate
ice cream cone,
it means you are not eating
strawberry.

But you accept the loss
in order to
enjoy
the chocolate.

You owe it to yourself
to focus on the ice cream
you have chosen."

— *Leaving the Fold* p. 523

I always had a terrible time making decisions as a JW. I think it was because Witnesses are trained to be meek and teachable. Docile, even. The biblical animal metaphor employed in talks is that we are sheep. We learned to follow implicitly the leadings of God's organization, and mistrust anything our treacherous heart and sinful flesh might say differently. You "wait on Jehovah"—which means don't do anything if no clear choice is indicated.

I remember visiting Corning Glass on a family trip. It was a cool place to tour as a kid. At the end, my parents said Susannah and I could each pick out a little glass figurine from the gift shop. They were maybe a quarter of an inch tall, little animals with a hundred beautiful facets. And I couldn't pick between two. I just couldn't, I loved them both. Even at nine years old or so, I had such a fear of missing out. I went out to the car bawling, with no figurine. My weary parents made a decision at some point in there and bought me both of the tiny figures. I still have them tucked away.

That experience has stuck with me all my life. My parents were pretty nice people. Yes, I later came to deeply rue various decisions they'd made—principally, which religion to join. For years, I harbored such bitterness about some of their choices. Every now and then, I still do. But to be real, they didn't sit down and say, "What can we do to make Phillip's life turn out as miserably as possible?" and then make that their guiding principle in life. They weren't trying to hurt me. Rather, their actions—and inactions—inadvertently caused damage.

But they loved me, and still do, I think it's safe to say. And honestly, the message of Jehovah's Witnesses has been honed over the decades to be extremely persuasive. After a certain point, it's almost impossible to say no. For my parents, it worked exactly as designed.

Work

THE SHRIMP WAS ALWAYS WHAT GOT ME. THOSE TRAYS OF SHRIMP cocktail set out on the festive red and green plastic tablecloth. Baby carrots and Bison-brand French onion dip sat beside the crock pot of Swedish meatballs and platters of rolled cold cuts. A pan of chocolate cherry cake was on the counter. Its thick, crusty icing would tilt and crack like lake ice in springtime as the knife sliced through it. It was Christmas Eve at the ski shop where I worked, and every year it closed early for the holiday dinner.

My family never ate shrimp. It wasn't a seafood thing; we ate a lot of fish. My mom made a great linguini with clam sauce. But I guess since we never had it, shrimp became different. It seemed like a delicacy for rich people. I've always craved it. Despite that, I never took a single one from the holiday platter. It was Christmas shrimp, forbidden by God himself as I understood it. If I took a shrimp, what might I do next? I would have opened the floodgates of sin.

"As with one person,

    also with a group or body of people, large or small,

        a **slight** deviation

            from right principles,

              if let run,

can cause

      gross lawlessness

      and

    incalculable trouble."

— *Watchtower* 01/01/75, p. 201

Work

It was a small family-owned sporting goods shop—bikes in the summer, skis in the winter. No one was getting rich there, but it paid the bills. I'd always loved riding my bicycle. When I turned sixteen, I applied to work as a bike mechanic. I'd had jobs mowing lawns and shoveling snow, but this was the first "real" job I'd gone for.

I didn't realize stores had preprinted job applications, so I had my dad help me write a resume. I carefully listed my work experience, such as it was. When I handed it to Bob, the repair shop manager, he looked it over and chuckled. "You had a little help with this, eh?" he said. He asked if I had any experience working on bikes. I admitted I only knew how to lube the chain. "Well, tell me how you do that," he responded. Evidently, I didn't sound like a complete nitwit, and he hired me on.

Working as a bike mechanic attracts some interesting characters. It doesn't require a degree, and there are no drug tests. Some are young guys like I was, working part-time after school. We spent almost our entire paycheck right back onto bike parts. Some are a little older, guys putting off college to be ski bums, race bikes, or smoke weed. One guy lived in an old bowling alley, next to a nudist colony he'd visit sometimes. He believed in cologne instead of showers. A pungent smell tended to linger when he'd leave the room.

There were usually a couple of older guys, too. They were former bike mechanics who returned to it after burning out on an assembly line, or they had just never left. One had his pilot's license and owned several apartment buildings. He seemed to work there just for fun.

After Bob found out I was a Witness, he enjoyed debating Bible topics with me. Eventually I felt outmatched by his sizable conversational skills. I ended up just handing him an entire book, *Reasoning from the Scriptures*. It was a reference Witnesses carried at the time to overcome objections while preaching. It was more of a JW-only book; you weren't supposed to give it out to people. But I respected him and felt it would answer his every question.

About a week later, he handed it back with a bemused expression. Since he'd been exposed to such a blast of pure JW reasoning power in the book, I was a bit surprised when he didn't fall at my feet like the biblical jailer of Acts 16 and beg me, "Sir, what must I do to get saved?"

It was a small shop; I think I was the first Witness ever to work there. I felt that at every moment, it was important to give a good impression of Witnesses. Sometimes it was easier said than done. The shop bathroom, for example, was papered with "Lange girl" posters: a ski industry tradition featuring models wearing ski boots and not much else.

And then there was the annual Christmas party. Each year I would studiously try to avoid the kitchen that day—a difficult task, since it was exactly in the middle of the store. I would stash my triple-decker peanut butter and jelly sandwich in the basement and eat it as I sat on a pile of ski boot boxes, while people grazed on the good stuff upstairs.

Not that chocolate cake and Swedish meatballs are evil. It was just the fact it was for Christmas. Any other day of the year I'd have been all over it. Christmas is an amalgam of customs taken from all over—the Romans, the Celts, most pre-Christian groups you can think of. It's a nominally Christian holiday now, but its origin story horrified early JWs when they checked into it. There is an old black-and-white photo in JW history books of Christmas dinner at Bethel headquarters. In the picture, Christmas presents sit by each seat. But that had ended decades before I came along.

"Christmas is securely rooted in a heap of **decayed pagan practices,** and hence the whole thing is a **stench** in the nostrils of ***true*** Christians."

- *Awake* 12/22/47, p. 11

Confusingly, JW articles take the exact opposite tack regarding the piñata, another custom with "pagan" origins.

"A main concern is, **not** what the practice meant *hundreds of years ago,* but how it is viewed **today** in your area."

- *Awake* 09/22/03, p. 24

It got a bit hard sometimes keeping track of which things were on the naughty vs. nice list. But since I didn't live in Mexico, there were no piñata parties at work, just Christmas parties. That made it simpler to follow the rules.

My dad's family are mostly dyed-in-the-wool Catholics, with a smattering of nuns and priests to spice things up. One of his aunts who was a nun faithfully sent her nephew a Christmas card with lottery tickets each year. It was a double whammy of badness—pagan holidays *and* gambling. Each year he would send it back with a long explanation of why Christians shouldn't be doing either one. She was as stubborn as he was. The annual exchange went on for years.

My parents were baptized as JWs when I was five and Susannah was two. That was the end of Christmas, birthdays, Mother's Day, Father's Day, Halloween, Thanksgiving, Easter, and pretty much any other holiday you can think of. It caused quite a rift between my dad and his mother; they didn't speak for several years. I recall a rare visit to her house when I was little. Things had gone south again, as they tended to do there. We walked out to the car as she stood in the doorway, railing against my parents for depriving us kids of Christmas and birthday presents.

I didn't feel deprived. My parents bought us things all the time, it seemed like. Once or twice we even tried having a "Present Day" when I was growing up. It was a gift exchange, set on a random day. But it felt forced, and we eventually gave it up.

At work, I never brought up that I was a Witness if I could help it. I just wanted to blend in. But everyone knew, and they'd bring it up sometimes. Jennifer worked in the clothing department while she finished her master's degree. One time she asked me what was so wrong with crosses. (JWs believe Jesus died on a stake, not a cross.)

"Well," I answered uncomfortably, checking to see if she had one around her neck. "Say it's what killed Jesus. It would be like someone shot your brother, and then you started wearing a little gun on a necklace. It doesn't make much sense."

"Mmm," she said noncommittally.

Tim, the sales manager, liked Eastern philosophy. He explained that every name people had for God over the millennia contained an "Ahh" sound. God, Brahma, Allah, Krishna, Yahweh, Shiva. "Ahh" was what you said when you're satisfied, comfortable. Jehovah fit the pattern, I realized. I didn't quite know what that meant.

I said "ah" all the time. It was a running joke in the shop. A person would assert something to me. "Ah," I'd say thoughtfully, an ambiguous expression that was my version of the Indian head bobble. I hadn't realized I was invoking Tim's ancient god-sound. For me, it was a neutral word which someone could interpret as me agreeing, if they wished. I was surrounded by non-JWs, and my beliefs were like a giant cube of granite. There was no wiggle room, no debate about what was right or wrong. "Ah" was my safety valve. It was the lubricant which allowed me to exist in this parallel universe without everyone hating me. It smoothed my interactions, like squirting powdered graphite in a sticky car lock.

I was supposed to hate my coworkers.

"We **hate** them,
not in the sense of
wanting to do them harm
or
wishing them harm
but in the sense of

avoiding them
as we would
poison
or a
poisonous snake,
for they can
poison us
spiritually."

- *Watchtower* 06/15/80, p. 8

But I didn't hate them, not really. I don't think many JWs do. What happens is you just become indifferent as to whether they live or die. Witnesses realize their lifestyle has a lot of downsides. They look forward to Armageddon as the time when the score will be evened out. Everyone gets their shot to become a JW. If they didn't, well, that's too bad. They had their chance.

"If he dies,

he dies."

- Ivan Drago
Rocky IV

Work

That outlook bled into my job later as a nurse. One time I had a patient who was dying from a fall. He was old, and his wife and I were in his room all night. I tried to keep him comfortable as he clung—surprisingly tenaciously—to life. The amount of meds I pushed through his IV probably would have knocked out a horse. He died just before dawn. His wife and I sat near the bed, both of us dry-eyed and exhausted.

Outside, the charge nurse had arrived minutes before for her day shift. Seeing the flatline on the monitor, she bustled in, tears rolling down her cheeks. She gathered the new widow in her arms. Not for the first time, I sensed my calibration was off. She had summoned more emotion over the man's death in three minutes than I had in twelve hours. I quit the job soon after. I needed a factory reset.

I've never worked a job with another Witness, except when I cleaned offices with a JW crew. But I needed no one to watch me to make sure I was being good. I policed myself. It's well summed up by the concept of a panopticon—a prison shaped like a circle. All the cells face into an open area. In the center is a guard tower with one-way glass, so the prisoners can't see the guard. Is he watching them that moment? You're not sure, so you have to behave just in case. The prison might even have no guard sometimes. But the panopticon design means the prisoners will behave anyway. You never know who is looking.

That's how it is as a JW: we make our own prison. It's why we don't have to live on a walled compound out in the boonies. If we're out and about, we take our prison walls with us. Jehovah is always watching. Another apt metaphor is the telescreen in George Orwell's *1984*. At any moment someone may be observing you, checking up on you. It might be another Witness. Or just Jehovah, up there tallying good deeds and bad deeds in his Big Book o' Deeds.

I read *1984* again not too long ago. The three slogans of Ingsoc—War is Peace, Freedom is Slavery, Ignorance is Strength—reminded me of JW teachings.

"*War Is Peace*"

"...Jehovah God
 is frequently spoken of not only as
 'the God of peace,'
  or
 'the God who gives peace,'
but also as
 'a manly person of war'
 and as
 'Jehovah of armies.'

To vindicate his sovereignty and to restore peace he finds it necessary at times to resort to war".

- *Watchtower* 08/15/66, p. 491, par. 1

To bring peace, Jehovah will wage war. When the organization occasionally speculates a bit about how many will survive Armageddon, they generally settle on the then-current number of JWs. It usually hovers around 0.1% of the world population. Ergo, to show his love for humans, God will destroy 99.9% of them.

"No, we are not speaking in self-contradiction." Watchtower 10/15/59, p. 622, par. 3

You might think that by now, the Creator of the universe would have come up with a solution more sophisticated than killing everyone. But evidently not quite yet.

<u>**"Freedom**</u>

<u>*is*</u>

<u>**Slavery"**</u>

"The world's **freedom** is a deceptive lie, for it results in **slavery** to sin and corruption."

- Watchtower 01/15/92, p. 29

Better to be a tractable slave of God. So how does a docile slave behave for his slave owner? JW leadership has given it some thought.

"Ponder a literal *slave-master* relationship.

Would a faithful, trusted **slave** put off **serving his master** or treat such **service** as of minor importance?

Would he give first attention to his own comforts or personal interests in life?

Most certainly not!"

- *Watchtower* 06/15/74, p. 372, par. 18

Hmm, so which servants of Jehovah are the best at it?

"There is no servant in the world as good as a good Colored servant, and the **joy** that he gets from rendering faithful **service** is one of the **purest joys** there is in the world."

- *Golden Age* 07/24/29, p. 702

Oh, Watchtower…Just…no. Nope nope nope.

"*Ignorance Is Strength*"

WORK

"It would be a mistake to think that **you need to listen to apostates** or to **read their writings** to refute their arguments. Their twisted, poisonous reasoning can cause spiritual harm and can contaminate your faith like rapidly spreading gangrene."

- *Watchtower* 02/15/04, p. 28

"'You see,' said Aslan. 'They will not let us help them...

Their *prison* is only in their own **minds,** yet they are in that prison;

and so afraid

of being taken in that they cannot be taken out.'"

- The Last Battle

"Ignorance

is

bliss..."

- "Ode on a Distant Prospect of Eton College"
Thomas Gray

It appears the JW organization has gone three for three on matching the policies of a fictional totalitarian police state! Tell 'em what they've won, Johnny! "Well, Bob, they've won total control of their followers. And a new washing machine!"

I stayed too long at that job, eight years. I got restless, but I was unsure what else to do. I stopped showing up to the unpaid mandatory meetings. So they fired me. Anyone could see it coming, but I didn't. I drove home in a daze on a Saturday morning.

I called my dad, and he picked me up so I could spend the rest of the morning preaching. It was a safe endeavor. I would never get fired from going door to door. As I climbed into the back seat and greeted the rest of the Witnesses, I leaned back and sighed: "Ahh."

Sex

"After this Adam was put into a deep sleep while God took from him that from which he could form an helpmeet for Adam.

This means that Adam at the first was a *bi-sexual* creature, and that God took away from him that **part** which would make the female."

- *Watchtower* 03/01/26, p. 77, par. 7

Sex

SO, APROPOS OF NOTHING, I'VE NOTICED SEX IS SLIGHTLY messed up for JWs. (Not that the sex they're having is messed up. I'm sure it's mostly missionary. Or is that only for missionaries? Do regular pioneer couples use a pioneer position? When a man is appointed to be a member of the Governing Body, is he briefed on a special Governing Body–only sex move? After all, both the words "body" and "member" are in the title. It's very racy. Although I could see how it might get a bit awkward, making eye contact with your fellow "members" across the boardroom table.)

One time when I was a teenager, we had some friends over who were much cooler than I was. They brought some of their CDs. Everyone asked what there was to listen to, and I started listing the album titles out loud. Suddenly I got completely flustered and blushed hard. (I blushed a lot in my younger years.) I mean, you couldn't really blame me. I'd never heard of the "Barenaked Ladies."

I didn't know what was going on. It was shocking to me that a good JW (as all our friends naturally were) would bring such a CD. Of course, I learned later on the band is actually very nice (as almost all Canadian things are). Eventually, I even owned some of my own Barenaked Ladies CDs. BMG music club, twelve CDs for the price of one.

The JW religion has a split personality when it comes to sex. Speakers are super explicit about sex at the Kingdom Hall, yet simultaneously everyone is super repressed about sexual matters. There is a constant flow of talks and *Watchtower* articles warning about sex of all sorts—adultery, fornication, oral sex, anal sex, pornography, and "porneia": a biblical Greek word for sexual uncleanness. Porneia is a conveniently vague term, applicable to whatever modern-day kink the Governing Body wants to come down on.

"Lap dancing is defined as

'an activity in which a usually seminude performer *sits and gyrates* on the lap of a customer.'

Depending on the facts of an actual situation, this could constitute **sexual immorality** requiring judicial action.

A Christian who has taken part in such activity should

seek help

from the elders."

- *Watchtower* 11/18, p. 27

After that article came out, I saw Facebook screenshots of sweet, innocent JWs from other countries. They were still trying to figure out what lap dancing was. Until then, they'd never heard of such a thing. No one can claim the *Watchtower* isn't educational. (As JWs like to say, reading Watchtower literature for four years is equal to a college education.)

One notable Sunday talk was themed "A Godly View of Sex and Marriage." Whenever it came up in the rotation, you knew you wouldn't be making much eye contact with the hapless speaker. Following the talk outline provided by the organization, he would explain in excruciating detail what it meant for husbands and wives to render to each other their marital due.

In one talk I gave, I included a long illustration depicting a person having lustful thoughts about a coworker, complete with inner monologue. As a twenty-year-old ministerial servant, I thought I was being edgy and sophisticated. (Ministerial servants are analogous to deacons; they assist the elders by handling various congregation tasks.) To my mind, I was giving a captivating talk which would maybe rattle someone in the audience who had been straying a bit from the straight and narrow. Looking back, I'm pretty sure I was just telling everyone where my *own* head was at work.

But the wild thing is how, since there's not any sort of Sunday School for JW kids, they're always in the auditorium sitting with their parents. From infancy, they're exposed to this constant stream of instruction-slash-dire-warnings about sexy times. The almost inevitable result: I ended up simultaneously very repressed about sex publicly, but the typical horny teenager privately.

Of course, I was very ashamed about these sexual thoughts—never mind masturbation, which I understood could turn you gay. I knew any slip-ups were on me. They meant I wasn't trying hard enough to follow the leading of the holy spirit. Time after time, I would gamely pit my willpower and desire to be godly against my teenage hormones, with predictable results.

"In fact, masturbation can lead into homosexuality.

In such instances the person, not satisfied with his lonely sexual activity, seeks a partner for mutual sex play.

This happens *much* more frequently than you may realize.

Contrary to what many persons think, homosexuals are **not** born that way, but their homosexual behavior is learned."

- *Your Youth- Getting the Best Out of It*
p. 39, par. 9-10

And porn! I became quite an aficionado. The early days of the J. C. Penny and Sears catalog underwear sections gave way to harder stuff. And by that, I of course mean books about pregnancy. My family never had cable TV—too much smut. But what we did do is go to the library every week. I found that the nonfiction section contained truly a wealth of prurient literature for a determined teenager. It was irresistible in those pre-Internet days.

Two sections in particular were my go-to areas. One was the social sciences section. It offered books, frequently illustrated, discussing various sexual and developmental topics. Another section was the art books. Lots of photography anthologies had tasteful nude portraits mixed in. I'm giving away all my trade secrets here. In an incident that mortified my early adolescent self, one day my mom found a long-overdue library book under my bed. It contained detailed—rather hirsute, as I recall—1970s-era black-and-white photos of the childbirth process. As with many kids raised in strict religious households, my sneaking-around skills would improve considerably, honed to a razor's edge in the years to come.

From time to time we'd visit my maternal grandma. She wasn't a Witness, and her attic offered an interesting selection of racy items. A paperback of *Valley of the Dolls*. *Cosmopolitan* magazines from the 1970s. (I first learned about a monokini by reading in her attic. Quite a revelation, since JW women are strongly discouraged from wearing anything except a modest one-piece swimsuit. Although, I guess a monokini *is* a one-piece. Loophole?)

If I were ever home alone, I'd try through the TV static to see if the afternoon soap opera had a love scene. I would check the neighbors' windows, hoping to catch a glimpse of underwear. What's that? Maladjusted, you say? Whatever do you mean? But that was about all I could do—that is, until the Internet came along.

I remember when I spent an astronomical two thousand dollars I'd saved up to build my own computer. I assembled it after studying the giant *Computer Shopper* magazine. I set it up in my room, the enormous CRT monitor strategically facing away from the door. While I didn't buy it specifically *for* porn, the temptation was irresistible. With my AOL disc, I'd fire up the ol' modem. And eventually, I saw pictures of naked women!

You had to watch the picture load layer by layer, tantalizingly blurry at first, until slowly the full glory was revealed. It was a bit like Proverbs 4:18, a favorite JW scripture to explain why teachings change over the years. To paraphrase, "the path of the righteous grows brighter, until the day is firmly established." Only in this case, an airbrushed body instead of a path.

As download speeds slowly increased, so did my porn consumption. I think it did for pretty much every male my age in the religion. I can't really speak to the effect on female JWs. Honestly (and as is the case in most fundamentalist Christian groups), the idea of female sexuality—that women might also want to masturbate and have orgasms—is largely a foreign concept to the all-male hierarchy.

When new Bethelites attend Bethel Entrants School, part of the curriculum is watching Bethel videos about sex. Leaked by anonymous Bethelites in 2018, the training videos have come to be known by the affectionate moniker "Pillowgate." (The name refers to the rather disturbing amount of time the videos—which are available on YouTube—spend in discussing how bad it might be to stimulate oneself against a pillow. Spoiler: very.)

They delve deeply into hypothetical scenarios of what constitutes porneia. For example, is it porneia when a dating couple grind for a bit on the dance floor? Yes, yes it is. On the other hand, two male Bethelites in the nude masturbating face to face? Not porneia. Not as bad. (It's good the Governing Body is there to sort all this out for us.)

The organization prepared two videos: one for men and one for women. The one for women is much shorter. The moderator (a man, of course) touches briefly on not looking at shirtless guys on Instagram. But most of the runtime is spent addressing the core problem with women—excuse me, that should of course read "the core problem *for* women"—tempting the poor men, who would have no problems staying chaste, if only it weren't for women flirting or dressing too provocatively.

"Of course,
a woman can be covered
from head to toe,

but

if she
walks
*in a **provocative** way,*

she would cease
to be modest."

— *Awake* 08/08/76 p. 25

One might think self-control on the part of the men should be a factor, and that this smacks of victim blaming. And I believe one would, indeed, be hitting the proverbial nail on the head. But for now suffice it to say that, for all intents and purposes, female sexuality is—at least when it comes to JW leadership—only considered in terms of how it affects male sexuality.

"Christian women have the **obligation** not to dress **provocatively,** not to **tempt** men to keep **looking** at them and so reap a **prideful** pleasure in noting how they are able to **play** upon the **emotions** of men."

- *Watchtower* 08/01/69 p. 463, par. 22

As in any large multi-national bureaucracy, the Society can take a while to get the gears turning. Its response to the porn problem was slow. Men at every level of the organization were falling prey: Bethelites, circuit overseers, elders, pioneers, you name it. The problem was, at that rate, if they all got in trouble and had to be demoted, there would be no one left to actually do all the work.

And so a veritable flood of counsel began about porn. There were articles for the congregation to study together, articles for young people, letters of counsel to the congregations. For years, every time the circuit overseer came around to visit the congregation and met with the elders and ministerial servants, he would bring up pornography.

Probably by necessity, porn was downgraded from a judicial matter (which generally ends in an announcement of either public censure, or excommunication if repentance seems lacking) to a matter for private counseling. The important thing was to confess. You had to tell the elders what you'd been getting up to. After all, only in this way could you receive their spiritual help and healing. After the initial counsel, you had the enjoyable arrangement of being checked up on regularly. You'd have to report whether you'd been a good Witness and were staying away from porn.

"Confiding in others will take courage and determination.

Yet, it is a vital step toward conquering the addiction and reconnecting with loved ones.

Susan, mentioned earlier, relates:

'Afterward, I felt a huge gush of relief. Those moments were *painful*, but they resulted in feelings of peace and approval.'"

- *Watchtower* 08/01/13, p. 7

Now I will admit that, in addition to the moral failing of the pornography itself, I never, ever turned myself in. Much like masturbation, I always felt like I *almost* had a handle on it. With just a few more months I'd be cured. I was sure of it. My deadlines always seemed to slip, but I stuck to my private plan.

I had a relative my age who had been caught by his wife looking at porn. It became supremely awkward. He lost all his privileges in the congregation ("privileges" meaning giving talks and generally taking the lead). Somehow the entire family knew about his "problem." It made for some weird dynamics at family dinners. My dad, as a long-time elder, made sure to counsel him one-on-one, on top of whatever his local elders were already doing.

Watching that play out cemented my conviction: I would take care of my own issues myself. And one day in my early twenties, I realized something. Even without weekly counseling, I no longer fixated on it like I had in my teenage years. One could almost think that the net result of all the talks about porn was, funnily enough, people thinking more about porn. It's like someone instructing you not to think about pink elephants. Invariably, you immediately start thinking about pink elephants.

Many JWs marry young so they can have sex. They aren't allowed to date casually (too much temptation to get frisky), don't have sex before marriage, and also aren't supposed to masturbate or look at porn. As a result, nineteen or twenty is a fairly common marriage age. I didn't go that route. My confidence and self-esteem always ran a mite low. I felt like I needed to level up a good bit before I'd be a passable husband.

Looking back now, I'm pretty relieved I didn't get married young. It could well have made things more complicated down the

Sex

road. I almost think that perhaps, subconsciously, I wanted to keep all the options open for future me.

I don't want to get too dark, but I often wonder whether all the sexual repression is a factor contributing to the child sexual abuse within the religion. Many Witnesses have had, at most, one sexual partner their entire life. They have the low self-esteem fundamentalist Christianity is so good at creating. ("Wow, you must have very low self-esteem," my mom would always coolly say if Susannah or I seemed impertinent.) The idea is that we're inherently sinful. We've fallen from the original perfection of Adam and Eve. If we do anything good, it's only thanks to Jehovah. And if we do something bad, it's just confirmation *we're* bad and need Jesus' ransom sacrifice.

But then this person has a child under their control in one way or another. They don't need to prove their worth to this child. The child is already under their influence, due to the difference in age and position in the family or congregation. Compliance with authority figures is built into JW doctrine, making grooming a child for sexual abuse an easy task.

And the thing I knew, but didn't really connect, is that JWs are super concerned with the reputation of Jehovah's organization. They never want to sully that reputation. If you do, you're bringing reproach on Jehovah's name. Instead of suing another Witness in court for some business problem, they generally follow the counsel of 1 Corinthians 6:7 to "rather let yourselves be wronged." Whatever it takes so outsiders see nothing bad that might turn them off from joining.

Of course, a lot of things JWs consider "bad" are perfectly legal in the world at large (i.e., sex without being married). So for things like that (and it's a long list), they've set up a separate, parallel judicial system within the congregation. Realistically, they feel this system isn't just parallel, it's superior. Because it's based on the Bible.

Doesn't it seem like it breaks down a bit when it comes to child abuse, though? That *is* illegal in society, but JWs still would prefer to handle it internally. Because if police don't know about any child molesters among JWs, there's no reproach on Jehovah's name. I think what Witnesses don't consider is this: the fact sex offenders exist in the JW ranks isn't in and of itself a reflection on the organization. A certain percentage of humans simply are pedophiles. I've seen the figure put at an upper limit of five percent. (Researchers do point out that the terms child molester and pedophile are not precisely interchangeable. Some people molest children without being pedophiles; conversely, not all diagnosable pedophiles molest children.) It's just simple math, then, that as in any group—Catholics, atheists, architects, Ivy League university employees—a small percentage of JW members are child molesters.

I know Witnesses would like to think people get a personality makeover when they become a Witness, and completely abandon all their bad tendencies. Unfortunately, studies have shown pedophiles don't lose their sexual interest in children over time. It doesn't matter whether the method is Bible study or more, shall we say, scientifically rigorous methods.

That means each congregation of a hundred publishers probably has one or two sex offenders. I think about that sometimes. I belonged to quite a few different congregations. I may well have known half a dozen child molesters over the years, unbeknownst to me.

The problem is, if abuse isn't reported to secular authorities (so as not to bring reproach on the organization), the mechanisms law enforcement has for tracking sex offenders, and bringing them to justice, cannot be set in motion. And the JW internal handling of child molesters is, let's be honest, woefully inadequate.

I've heard many rather unimportant announcements during congregation meetings. Which group will be cleaning the hall this week. Not to touch the thermostat. (Thermostat control is a surprisingly big issue.) Don't wear too much perfume in the hall. Who will be feeding the visiting Sunday speaker. But never, ever, would it be announced So-and-so had abused a child, and for everyone to watch out around them. Never, never, never.

I'm not sure exactly why that is. I think it's connected to elders feeling obliged in some sense to not drag the person's name through the mud. They feel like he has paid his penalty in the JW judicial process. I think it also has to do with preserving the layers of confidentiality and secrecy in the organization.

And so a curious situation has arisen. It's much like the curse of the monkey's paw, which I cheerfully admit I first learned about from watching *Adventure Time* (season five, episodes one and two). In their burning desire to avoid bringing reproach on Jehovah's name and organization, JW leadership has created an organization which *is* bringing reproach on Jehovah's name. The neat, clean, law-abiding reputation hides a serious problem of child sexual abuse.

(Incidentally, you would think if Almighty God was truly worried about what puny humans thought of him, he has the wherewithal to step in and take care of his own reputation. The fact that he hasn't means perhaps *we* shouldn't worry too much about it, either.)

"Everything

looks

perfect

from

far

away"

- "Such Great Heights"
  The Postal Service

As abuse survivors gather the courage to come forward, the spotlight is shifting from the largest institutions, notably the Catholic Church, to smaller groups like Jehovah's Witnesses and the Boy Scouts. In fact, the 2015 "Australian Royal Commission into Institutional Responses to Child Sexual Abuse" examined scores of organizations in that country.

When they turned their attention to Jehovah's Witnesses, the commission found that the names and case details of more than one thousand members investigated by congregation elders for child sexual abuse since 1950 had been passed on from local congregations to Australia's Bethel branch office. Everything had been carefully recorded in confidential JW files. However, not a single one had been reported to authorities. Congregation members had not been warned in an announcement that these individuals were dangerous to children.

If someone is publicly reproved or disfellowshipped (excommunicated), the elders would historically make an announcement saying, "So-and-so has been reproved/disfellowshipped from the congregation." The reason is not made public. It's left to the listener to wonder if it was for smoking cigarettes, sexually abusing children, accepting a blood transfusion, or murder. Curiously, all these actions are equally weighted by JWs when it comes to how wrong they are.

Nowadays, the announcement is an even more vague "So-and-so is no longer one of Jehovah's Witnesses." This leaves it unclear whether the person left due to profound disagreements with the doctrine, or has been sexing it up on the town. You can imagine which scenario most JWs will assume is the correct one.

Compared to Australia's branch office, the United States branch oversees more than seventeen times the number of Witnesses. So, presumably, it also has a proportionally larger number of child molesters in its records. As more details continue to come to light, people aware of it are understandably turned off from wanting to join. That, along with the general decline in religion's importance in the Western world, probably helps explain why growth is flat in so many countries for Jehovah's Witnesses.

Unlike many fundamentalist religions, the JW organization has historically been a bit down on members having kids. It tended to recommend that couples remain childless. In this way, they would be unencumbered and more readily available for organization assignments.

However, there have been decreasing conversion rates from public preaching in recent years. This has led to a corresponding shift in focus to growth from within. The children of JWs are the most likely prospects to continue growing the religion.

"It is easier for us to be molded into conformity with Jehovah's Word if that Word is brought to bear upon us while we are young instead of waiting till we are old and more set in our ways.

The young are more pliable, and the younger the better."

- *Watchtower* 01/15/54
p. 53, par. 17

One effect has been on the age at which young Witnesses are encouraged to get baptized. Taking their cue from Jesus, who waited until he was thirty years old to get dunked, JWs long advised that a person be old enough to make a well-informed decision, fully aware of all that baptism as one of Jehovah's Witnesses signifies. However, the recommended age range has gradually drifted down over time. Witnesses now focus more on the preteen years.

Sex

"As soon as she learned to
read and write,

        Paola enrolled in the
        Theocratic Ministry School

and became a publisher.

Because of her love for Jehovah,
she got baptized at the age of

                      seven."

          - *Yearbook* 2011, p. 58

Growth

"Timothy,

    guard what has been
             entrusted to you,

turning away from the
    empty speeches
      that violate what is holy

and from the
    contradictions of the
      falsely called 'knowledge.'

By making a
    show
      of such
    knowledge,
      some have *deviated* from the faith."

           - 1 Timothy 6:20-21

CAN I JUST SAY, THE BIBLE CHARACTER TIMOTHY WAS MY MAIN man. He was a young single guy, progressing up through the ranks, trying to help the congregations. That was just like me. Actually, he had it harder—his dad wasn't a Christian. Although on the other hand, he had the apostle Paul helping him, so I guess it all evens out. But man, when Paul circumcised Timothy so it wouldn't stumble Jewish people—how awkward would that be. Oh, and the pain. Ay Dios mio.

Wait, is "stumbling someone" another JW-only phrase? It means doing something someone else gets offended at. It's used as a way to shut down stuff people do which teeeeechnically isn't forbidden, but goes against JW norms. Like if a guy starts growing his sideburns too long, or a woman's skirt length creeps above the knee.

My dad had a Sunday talk he often gave in various congregations which discussed dress and grooming. I heard it so many times it's forever burned in my brain. He would talk about JW women going shopping. "When you try on an outfit, don't just stand at the mirror. Do you *pause* sit down? Do you *pause* bend over?"

"Will girls dressed in
    tight-fitting blue jeans
        and
      form-fitting sweaters
  make good wives?

Will boys dressed in
    skin-tight jeans
     and
  jackets with
      ornamental lacing
    and
leather buttons
    make good husbands?

    One cannot help but wonder."

- Awake 02/22/60 p. 9

He had a hard time coming up with much to say for men. JW speakers in recent years have focused on the crucial issue of suit pants being too tight. When I was a kid, my dad would warn men about "Hall and Oates" suits. As I understood it, they were suit jackets that stopped at the waist and had a diagonal opening in front. I think they were a thing for about a minute in 1980s music videos.

One time a group of us were out preaching. It was one of those lazy, sticky midsummer days, and we were in a minivan with no air conditioning. Steph, a twenty-ish young pioneer, sighed and abruptly hiked her skirt up way above her knees. (It seems to be less strict now, but in the 1990s JW women always had to wear pantyhose.) She was roasting, but her sister Amy was shocked. She told her to pull her skirt back down. The heat made Steph truculent, and she argued.

"Why?" she said. "I wear shorts this short."

She turned to me.

"Am I stumbling you?"

"No-o-o," I stuttered out, trying to look anywhere besides her legs.

Amy shot her sister the glare of death, and with one final, exaggerated sigh, Steph pulled her skirt back down.

"Skirts and the like should fit smoothly to middle of buttocks, then flow down, not hugging, touching or cupping...

Skirt length appropriate to leg if just skims back of leg where calf begins to curve in. (About one to two inches below the knee.) However, many women are more comfortable with a lower hemline."

- Awake 11/22/84 p. 23

Even when you're not preaching or at a meeting, you have to be thinking about it.

"Therefore, we should give attention to our **dress and grooming** while in the convention city, **including when we check in at the hotel.** Arriving in *shorts and a T-shirt* would **not** reflect **dignity."**

— *Our Kingdom Ministry*
04/12, p. 5, par. 6

So for sure, Paul's two letters to Timothy were ones I checked out a lot. My shields were always up, ready to deflect any empty speeches or falsely called knowledge. As they always said at the meetings, just a drop of poison in a glass of water would poison the entire thing. I could never let my guard down.

Once in a while a householder would say, "I'll take your literature if you take some from my church." Every JW knew what to say, wisdom passed down from one publisher to another. "Well, when you come knock on my door, then I'll take yours." Sometimes they'd take me up on it. "Okay, what's your address?" To which I'd respond with something along the lines of, "That would be cheating. You need to find me by canvassing the entire city, as I did you."

At least once I do remember taking their pamphlet, arguing that the ends justified the means. As I walked down the driveway, I crumpled it up in my hand. I wanted to make sure no poison leaked out. No doubt the householder was doing the same thing after he shut the door. Both of us thought we'd accomplished something.

What I didn't realize at the time is that the great danger lay not in someone standing up and making a bombastic speech denouncing my beliefs. Rather, it was in a thousand tiny interactions with people who weren't Witnesses.

The Achilles' heel of JWs when compared to, say, a cult sequestered on some compound in New Mexico, is that they have to go out and about every day, mingling with the world. There are ways to mitigate it. Many JWs are self-employed, or work for other JWs. One married couple in my congregation had a sizable office cleaning business. I worked for them for a while. We went to the businesses in the evening after they closed, and worked only with other Witnesses. Rarely did I ever have to interact with nonbelievers.

But many other Witnesses work jobs requiring them to spend all day with coworkers of other faiths. Some JWs I knew were bank tellers. Susannah was a dental assistant. I had a variety of jobs over the years: bike mechanic, security guard, nurse's aide, nurse.

Come to find out, those pagan heathens I worked with—who all evidently deserved to die at Armageddon if they didn't become JWs—were actually rather nice people on the whole. They were kind. They seemed to have no grand schemes to make a defiant stand against God.

That surprised me. As a well-taught JW, I had thought the prevailing personality trait of anyone not a Witness was defiance. The pictures in the magazines are filled with angry worldly people (except when they're replaced with seemingly nice coworkers, who are actually just trying to get in your pants). I was taught church steeples—and even the cross itself—are actually phallic symbols defiantly thrust up by ministers, like a middle finger toward God's nose. Hence, why Kingdom Halls have neither.

"Is there any real difference

in the practice of
parents today
who place a
necklace with a cross on it
around the
necks of their children

and the practice of
ancient Roman parents
who put a
necklace with a phallus on it
around the
necks of their children,

since
the cross
was a symbol of
the phallus?"

- Awake 07/22/64, p. 10

But it turned out non-Witness people were generally just folks minding their own business. They were simply trying to make a good life for their family. Working as a registered nurse, I found out a lot of nurses are caring deep down, but tend to get a little crunchy on the outside. Twenty-three-year-old petite nurses nonchalantly drop F-bombs left and right. I cringed a bit to hear them. To tell you the truth, there were a couple of nurses I didn't even really like. One in particular was constantly sneaking off to smoke. It was plainly against the rules. And let me tell you, I cherished rules. Scrupulously following every rule was the key to success as a good JW.

But if her patient was circling the drain, even that smoky RN could turn on a competence and concern which would make me completely comfortable having her as my nurse. It was as if people could have more than one dimension. Instead of being "bad" or "good" they had some of each. That was really messing with my head, you know? Because if they were mostly good with a little bad, was it okay for God to kill them at Armageddon? Wouldn't that make Jehovah a little bad? And what about children on that day of judgment?

"It is a serious time for **children** as well as adults,

because
children that do not obey Jehovah
will **not** be among the survivors of that battle.

God will not preserve them into his new world
merely because they are children.

This is evident from the fact that
he did not preserve the young children
through the flood of Noah's day
just because they were **children**.

It is also shown in the book of Ezekiel that
just because
you are
young
is
no reason
for God's keeping you
alive.

Ezekiel wrote: *'Slay utterly*
the old man,
the young man
and the virgin, and
little children
and women;

but come not near any man
upon whom is the mark.'
(Ezekiel 9:6, American Standard)"

- *Watchtower* 08/15/62, p. 495, par. 26

It takes some real pretzel twists of logic to explain why God could kill a whole school playground filled with children, and that would be righteous and loving. If anyone else did it, we would call them a mass-murderer and a psychopath.

In fact, it's not hard to follow JW reasoning down an even stranger path. JW theology holds that anyone executed at Armageddon by Jehovah has received his or her final judgment. However, most anyone who dies *prior* to Armageddon (except those who commit the rather nebulous "sin against the holy spirit") will be resurrected afterward for a do-over.

Following this to its logical conclusion, killing someone now is actually a good thing. Their death this side of Armageddon gives them an automatic pass into paradise. Rather than mourning each school shooting, JWs should be rejoicing. The shooter saved those children from a permanent execution by God.

This line of reasoning led to tragic consequences in 2018. A former JW named Lauren Stuart shot and killed her family and herself in Keego Harbor, Michigan. She was struggling with depression, fears about Armageddon, and ostracism from her Witness family since leaving the religion. Her final text explained, "I took my husband and kids with me so they don't have to feel my selfish act. They will sleep until Christ resurrects them" (Baldas, 2018). Fortunately, I don't think many JWs have considered the full ramifications of these teachings.

But little by little, I came to find there were many basically good people in the world. It was like Wesley in *The Princess Bride*. He spent years building up an immunity to the poison called iocane powder. I was unconsciously building a resistance to Watchtower dogma which constantly reiterated that everyone except JWs are bad.

One time a woman I worked with invited me to go skiing with her. She was much older than me and was simply a friendly soul. I went, but I felt uneasy about spending time alone with her (albeit at a ski resort filled with people). After all, I read about these sorts of situations all the time in the literature. Was she just trying to seduce me, an innocent young buck? It turned out I was rather overestimating my irresistibility to women. I didn't realize that people outside my religion could also have morals, that they too valued faithfulness to their spouse. The only thing that transpired was a pleasant day of skiing.

When my parents found out, they had a serious talk with me about the dangers of spending time alone with a woman. In fact, if I ever gave a Witness woman a ride home from a meeting, just the two of us, she would sit in the back seat to avoid any hanky-panky. Perhaps even more importantly, it avoided the *appearance* of any hanky-panky if another JW were to see us.

Some of my coworkers I got to know and respect were LGBTQ. Once again, I found that things did not quite seem to be the way they had been explained by the Watchtower organization. As I watched them save lives day after day, I weighed them against convicts on death row. There seemed to be a slight difference in what the two cohorts had done for the community. It was a bit difficult to see how, as JW doctrine asserts, the gay ICU nurse merited the death penalty equally with the serial killer. (The June 8, 1976 *Awake* hastily clarifies on page eleven, "Of course, it is up to God and his glorified Son to execute any such death penalty at the proper time.") The organization is candid when discussing its stance on sexual orientation.

"All those who, like scavenger **dogs** of the streets, practice *disgusting* things such as sodomy and lesbianism are debarred from gaining everlasting life in God's new system of things."

- *Watchtower* 05/15/70, p. 316

As in many conservative faith traditions, there is no path available to be both JW and openly gay. (The same holds true for transgender persons.) Same-sex attraction, to Jehovah's Witnesses, is a choice. As the aforementioned issue of *Awake* declares on page twelve, "People are 'gay,' then, because that is what they *want*" [italics theirs]. Over the years, the organization has explored what might cause such same-sex attraction, in hopes of then reversing the process for JWs struggling to meet the religion's requirements.

"The book *Making Your Family Life Happy* [also published by Jehovah's Witnesses] says: 'The influence of the father's masculine qualities can make a vital contribution to the development of a rounded-out, balanced personality.' A boy also needs acknowledgment, love, and approval from his father. (Compare Luke 3:22)

What can result when a father fails to give his child this needed attention? Emotional distress. Mental-health writer Joseph Nicolosi claims that male homosexuality is 'almost always the result of problems in family relations, particularly between father and son.'"

- *Awake* 02/08/95, p. 16

In addition to citing its own book as a reference, the organization here turned to a—as they ambiguously term him—"mental-health writer" named Joseph Nicolosi to bolster their position. Dr. Nicolosi, who died in 2017, was a psychologist and leading proponent of "reparative therapy," which can purportedly repair the problems that led to feelings of same-sex attraction. (Although the Watchtower Society has never pulled any punches in expressing its dislike for the Catholic Church, it did not seem to be a problem that Dr. Nicolosi was Catholic and worked out of the Thomas Aquinas Psychological Clinic in California. Any port in a storm, as they say.) In 1992, Nicolosi and two colleagues who were psychiatrists founded the National Association for Research and Therapy of Homosexuality (NARTH). The organization promoted conversion therapy as a way to change sexual orientation.

Dr. George Rekers, a psychologist and Southern Baptist minister, served as one of NARTH's board members. He resigned in 2010, after media outlets reported he had hired a male prostitute to accompany him on a two-week vacation in Europe. In 2012, California banned the use of conversion therapy on minors, labeling it as pseudoscience. Twenty states currently have similar laws. In 2019, Amazon stopped selling Nicolosi's books on its website.

"From Our Readers:

> 'Thank you for your article "The Homosexual Life-Style- Just How Gay Is It?" [March 22, 1986] Serving Jehovah, I now have a clean conscience, and I don't worry anymore about the harmful effects and insecurities that I feared a few years ago. Your article reassured me that the gay life-style isn't so gay and that true happiness is found by serving Jehovah God.'
>
> A. G., California

'I have homosexual feelings that are contrary to what Jehovah approves. I've been to my share of specialists, so-called Christian and non-Christian alike. They cannot understand why I do not simply give in to my desires. It's simple- I love Jehovah.

Coping with these desires is very difficult- sometimes it seems almost impossible- but it can be done. The question I had to ask myself was: 'Whom do I love more, Jehovah or myself?' I chose Jehovah. (Matthew 22:37) I am happier now, having kept my love and loyalty for Jehovah, than when I loved myself more.

My message to those who fight those feelings is this: If you love God as you keep saying you do, you'll learn to rely on his love and strength and not on your own love for pleasure.'

C. J., Montana"

- *Awake* 07/22/86 p. 28

Knowing the strict JW view of sexual orientation as disseminated by the Governing Body, it is intriguing to read the *Watchtower* magazine's 1963 autobiographical article about Ewart Chitty. After many years spent helping to oversee the organization's work in Britain, Chitty was appointed to the Governing Body in 1974. He would go on to resign just five years later, one of a small handful of men to have done so over the decades.

GROWTH

"With an older brother

        and a boy friend

    I attended some talks
        being given by the Bible Students,
as Jehovah's Witnesses were then known...

    Then, too, I have had
        the same friend and roommate
for the past thirty years or more,

        Brother Edgar Clay,
      whose life story
          you may have already read;

but now we share a lovely room,
        a most pleasant home
    with a fine view facing south,

        and an extra window
      looking out to rising fields and trees
          and the setting sun in all its glory."

- *Watchtower* 02/15/63, p. 120

I think what really helped push me a bit closer to the exit was the issue of blood transfusions. Based on their interpretation of Leviticus 17:14 and especially Acts 15:29, JWs refuse blood transfusions.

"For the holy spirit and we ourselves
   have favored adding no further burden to you
      except these **necessary** things:

to keep abstaining

   from things sacrificed to idols,
   ## from blood,
   from what is strangled,
   and from sexual immorality.
If you carefully keep yourselves
   from these things,
      ## you *will* prosper.

      ## Good health to you!"

- Acts 15:28-29

My whole RN career was spent with trauma patients. Let me tell you, we gave a lot of blood. JWs often imagine physicians as characters just itching for an opportunity to transfuse blood. That you have to keep your guard up, so they don't slip you a free unit of blood with your flu shot. In truth, it irks physicians to give blood.

From what I've observed, many doctors almost keep a little mental scorecard, and giving blood goes in the loss column. They feel that giving blood is the lazy way out, that a true practitioner of the art of medicine can get the job done using more cerebral methods. Hospitals make their job harder by requiring them to justify each unit in writing as they order it. But in my little nursing sphere, it was clear: blood saved lives.

"We do not want to die.

But

if we tried to

save

our present life

by breaking God's law, we would be in danger of

losing

everlasting life.

We are **wise**, then, to put our trust in the rightness of God's law,
with

full confidence

that **if we die** from any cause,
our Life-Giver

will remember us

and restore to us in the resurrection

the precious gift of life."

-What Does the Bible Really Teach?
p. 131, par. 15

I remember a skinny young kid, maybe fifteen, who came into the ICU after an accident. He improved rapidly over the next couple of days, and soon was able to transfer out to a regular floor. Several uneventful days passed, but then something in his belly started rebleeding. His nurse found him white as a sheet. He quickly lost consciousness, and soon after that his heart stopped. There simply wasn't enough blood in his vessels to pump. The nurses started CPR, and he was rushed back down to the ICU.

Blood transfusions started being pumped in incredibly quickly (seriously, a rapid infuser machine can dump two units of blood—roughly 800 mL—into an IV in about a minute). The team continued CPR until his heart restarted. He was then immediately taken to the operating room so the leak could be fixed. The unanswered question was whether he'd sustained a severe brain injury from the lack of oxygen while his heart was stopped.

I took care of him a few days later. He was responding a bit slowly to questions, but he knew his name and where he was. That was a great sign, and you could tell that with a little time, he'd be back at one hundred percent. There is no doubt that kid would have suffered a devastating brain injury, and in all likelihood be dead, without rapid infusion of blood. I saw similar situations almost every week. And after a while, I started to wonder why Jehovah would forbid a life-saving treatment.

"I, Jehovah, am your God, the One teaching you to **benefit** yourself."

- Isaiah 48:17

That verse kept nagging at me. I couldn't really think of another instance where following Jehovah's laws in the Bible would kill you. (God's enemies might kill you, but that wasn't God's fault.) It was always stressed in discourses that the law code given to Israel through Moses was far ahead of its time. In general, it handled health issues like quarantine and burying human waste correctly. So the ban on blood transfusions didn't seem to go with everything else. My pal the apostle Paul had told Timothy, "Keep holding the pattern of healthful words that you heard from me" (2 Timothy 1:13). The blood teaching just didn't fit with the pattern of Jehovah's other commands.

If it wasn't the Bible that was wrong, was the issue the JW interpretation of those verses? In the Gospels, Jesus himself had been challenged as to whether it was wrong to heal someone on the Sabbath, a day on which no work was to be done. He raised the example that a man was certainly allowed to rescue an animal which fell in a pit on the Sabbath. How much worthier it was to heal a human, even if it broke the rules (Matthew 12:11). Later, I learned that this principle of overruling biblical law to preserve human life is called "pikuach nefesh" by the Jewish community. I will forever mispronounce it as Pikachu nefesh.

It was hard for me to imagine a JW teaching could be wrong. But that was more reasonable than the Bible itself being in error. Even the organization explains that each word in the Bible is divinely inspired, whereas their literature is only guided by holy spirit—one step down. The situation reminded me of Sherlock Holmes' words that once you eliminate the impossible, whatever remains—no matter how improbable—must be the truth. There was no particular moment I said, "Aha! This religion is malarkey!" It was just something I filed away and tried not to think about. But quietly it festered.

Cognitive dissonance is a phrase which often comes up when talking about leaving an all-encompassing religion or group. It's when you learn something which breaks the worldview you've always known, but leaving that worldview behind is inconceivable. So you try and stuff the contradiction down in between the couch cushions of your brain. Hopefully it will just go away, or something.

"Close your eyes

   for your eyes will only tell the truth

   and the truth isn't what you want to see

   In the dark it is easy to pretend

   that the truth is   what   it   ought   to   be"

               - "The Music of the Night"
                   Phantom of the Opera

However, I had another chink in my armor. I'd joined a foreign-language group. The Watchtower organization has promoted the idea of learning a second language in recent years. The English territory is, frankly, kind of played out. It's been preached to for over a century. It wasn't uncommon to hear JWs say, "We're scraping the bottom of the barrel" regarding people getting baptized these days. Of the small number of new converts, a large percentage seemed to have mental or psychological issues they were trying to overcome.

The preaching work was honestly fairly dull, since it was so hard to "bring someone into the truth," as Witnesses call getting a person to the point of baptism. My family had collectively spent over one hundred years preaching, and none of us had a single convert. In contrast, the foreign-language groups were far more exciting. You were talking to people who perhaps had never been exposed to JWs before. They hadn't formed prejudices against them. Some of these populations consisted mostly of new immigrants who were appreciative of any assistance and interest shown toward their families. Groups sprouted in Spanish, Russian, Mandarin, American Sign Language, and a dozen other tongues.

Spanish was my group. There was a local Caucasian elder who had grown up in South America. Later, he'd been assigned to Central America as a graduate of the Ministerial Training School (the two-month course for single men). He conducted the language classes, and the small local Spanish-language group, which had limped along for years as part of an English-language congregation, was soon promoted to its own full-fledged congregation.

There were some hard-core JWs in the group. One older couple was Cuban and had fled Castro's crackdown on the Witnesses decades earlier. They had exciting stories of smuggling *Watchtower* magazines under the government's nose while JWs were banned.

Going preaching became much more interesting. We would scour the city directory for Spanish-sounding names. Then we might drive by the house to see if there was a Puerto Rico–flag air freshener hanging from the car's rear-view mirror. Or maybe there would be a satellite TV dish, which could mean they were getting international channels. Sometimes we would just go to the door and ask whoever answered if they knew of any Spanish-speaking people in the neighborhood. It got a bit stalker-ish sometimes.

Some of the best results we got were among undocumented immigrants working on dairy farms in the area. These guys were incredibly hard working, usually living with a bunch of other workers in a grimy trailer the farm owner provided. They were very humble and friendly. (As another plus for me, they were mostly from Mexico, and didn't talk as fast as the Witnesses I knew from Cuba and Puerto Rico. I had a fighting chance to keep up in a conversation with them.)

Undocumented immigrants were in a weird spot as JWs. We weren't going to turn them in. They could get baptized. But they weren't allowed any congregation privileges, because technically they were breaking the law. At one point, a minor scandal erupted in a congregation an hour or so north of us. A JW was speeding while out preaching. He got pulled over, and a couple of the Witnesses in the car were undocumented. They were detained and deported back to Mexico.

The organization has been really pleased to see the numerical growth in foreign-language sectors. However, what I don't think they totally thought through was the effect moving to a foreign-language congregation would have on JWs making the jump. It wasn't too hard to pick up the basics of Spanish. But for me, much of the nuance was lost. Giving talks was especially frustrating. In English, I could pick from half a dozen synonyms to give the exact sense I wanted to convey. Spanish was much different. Sure, I could explain the gist of a point. But all the finesse I felt made me a good speaker was gone. Although the Latino Witnesses were incredibly gracious, I knew the talks had to be fairly boring for them.

Studying the literature was similarly difficult. It felt like there was a veil between my brain and the full meaning of what was written. I had to have the English and Spanish editions side by side if I wanted to really understand the full sense of the writing. Instead of mulling over the minutiae of the articles, all my time was taken up just understanding the basics of what was written.

In this way, my tight connection to the organization gradually slackened somewhat. I was unplugged to a degree I hadn't been since I'd first learned to read. My mind wandered more easily at meetings. Questions I'd often mused about rolled around my brain more insistently. Did Jehovah *really* answer prayers? Because I'd never seemed to get any response. Why was it we could celebrate wedding anniversaries, but not birthdays? What exactly was bad about celebrating Thanksgiving? After all, the Israelites had harvest festivals. Why was it okay to wear wedding rings, if possibly they—like Christmas—had pagan origins?

"You try and pray

You memorize the lies

What you had before, but you're slippin'"

- "I Said You Were Lucky"
Dead Sara

Growth

My interpersonal skills had always been a bit wobbly, and for me the social aspect of JWs was never a strong suit. My sister and dad were so good in that department. They made friends easily, and spent convention intermissions seeing friends old and new. I was more like my mom, more comfortable with books and movies. For myself, the intermissions were just uncomfortable periods I had to try and fill between what *I* liked best, the talks and interviews. Moving to a foreign-language congregation had only served to add yet another layer of complexity to making small talk.

I wasn't much of a dancer either. You'll laugh, but it's a key skill for a Spanish-language JW. My white boy hip joints just didn't have the knack. The door-to-door preaching was another thing I wasn't too good at. I never had much going on in the way of Bible students, as potential converts are called.

I was more or less on the track to become a congregation elder. However, as a ministerial servant, one step below that, I had essentially all the responsibility I wanted. I could give talks during the week and even on Sunday. I oversaw the literature department. I did the congregation's accounting.

To become an elder only seemed to add unwanted jobs—shepherding the congregation, conducting judicial committees. I'd never had any desire to be a boss, to flex my authority over others. I feel bad even writing that, because I know how privileged I was as a male. The opportunities for a woman in the organization are incredibly limited. But that's just how I felt. What I enjoyed was doing research to prepare an interesting talk, giving the talk, and then fading into the background until I was needed again. I felt like Batman, if Batman's superpower was giving TED talks.

All this to say that, while I was devoted to Jehovah's Witnesses, it wasn't like some JW families that are four generations deep and deeply intermarried in local congregations. I kept my footprint light. Eventually, I moved about an hour away to a different Spanish-language congregation closer to my job at the time. My network of friends thinned a bit more. My parents and sister, the only other JWs in my family, had moved halfway across the country. We weren't in particularly close contact. The cognitive dissonance continued to quietly make itself known, and my doubts slowly grew more insistent.

As I think back on that time, it's actually a bit difficult to remember all the details. I felt foggy, like I was sliding into a funk. I was unhappy staying in an organization I'd started to think had some serious errors in its doctrine. But the thought of actually leaving made me equally miserable. I knew the rifts it would create with my family and the only friends I had, all JWs.

Talking with someone about it was not an option. Broaching my misgivings to any Witness would have been like walking into a minefield. JWs are trained to report anyone who raises subversive thoughts like that. The last thing I wanted was to be called into a judicial committee for apostasy. (An apostate is a Witness who leaves due to disagreements with theology.)

At the time, I had no inkling there was an ex-JW online community, or that books by ex-JWs like *Crisis of Conscience* existed. Living within the carefully curated JW bubble, I knew of not a single person that had ever left for purely doctrinal reasons. I felt absolutely alone. Despite all that, staying in felt more and more uncomfortable. My heart just wasn't in it anymore. A decision eventually coalesced: I would leave the religion.

"I'm wide awake

  And now it's clear to me

That everything you see

    Ain't always what it seems

  I'm wide awake

    Yeah, I was dreaming for

          so
        long"

- "Wide Awake"
Katy Perry

The title of the Watchtower Society's second main journal, after the *Watchtower* magazine itself, is "*Awake!*" complete with exclamation point. I was never quite clear what tense or sense the word "awake" was meant to have. But after joining the Spanish-language congregation, I learned the magazine in that language is called "*¡Despertad!*" It is a word of command, what you'd urgently tell your children when you discover their alarm didn't go off on a school day: "Wake up!"

I would catch myself chuckling and talking to the Society in my head. "Don't worry, Watchtower. I'm awake now." It reminded me of a story Holly would tell. (Holly was the Witness who raised all the objections when JWs who didn't know her came to her door.) She said after her parents got divorced, her mom would dance around the house, belting out "I Will Survive."

When it comes to leaving Jehovah's Witnesses, the strategy of "fading" is frequently recommended by the ex-JW community. Fading means quietly slipping out the back door, as opposed to formally writing a letter to your local elders explaining that you no longer wish to be a JW. The letter-writing process is termed "disassociation" by the organization. For some, disassociating feels like still playing by JW rules, and they are done with that. For others, writing such a letter of resignation is an essential part of moving on. And there is nothing inherently wrong with such action. Indeed, it's the bog-standard way to depart your average job, club, or organization. The trouble is that, unlike most churches, there is no simple, dignified way to leave the JW organization.

"The village believes the island gives us what we need"

Chief Tui:

"and no one leaves"

- "Where You Are"
Moana

Anyone who leaves of her own volition is scary to the leadership. Picture a disgruntled CEO who was fired, has a book deal, and never signed a nondisclosure agreement. Her old company would be terrified. So the JW organization's instruction to its adherents is clear: shun any disassociated person. Cut them off from your family. It serves two purposes. First, to help dissuade anyone who might be thinking about leaving. And second, to quarantine the person, so their apostate thinking doesn't spread to other active JWs.

Fading helps avoid those consequences. Here's the basic idea. You move to a new congregation that doesn't know you, ideally in a different city than your family and friends. You attend a couple of meetings. Then steadily reduce your attendance to zero. Your former congregation assumes you're going to the new one. The new one quickly forgets you ever moved there. Your family may be bummed that you've gotten so "spiritually weak," but they hopefully won't feel too much obligation to treat you like you're dead to them.

I'd never heard of "fading" at that point, but I came up with a very similar plan to leave. For me, the main obstacle was disentangling myself from all my congregation assignments. What with undocumented immigrants and a smaller candidate pool, any man in a Spanish-language congregation who has all his boxes ticked will have lots of talks and responsibilities. When I asked to "step down," that is, resign from being a ministerial servant, it was right as a circuit overseer's visit was coming up. The local elders wanted me to meet with him first.

The last thing I wanted to do was meet with the higher-ups. But at least it was an old-school Latino man, not a young white guy who might know a bit too well what I was thinking. We met in a side room of the hall after the meeting.

As I explained in my not-very-fluent Spanish how I had gotten kind of burned out and needed to take a break, his expression became grimmer. His questions were not really ones expressing concern and how he could help. Rather, they got right to the point: was I having doubts about the organization? I protested (lying through my teeth) that was not the case at all. I just needed to slow down a bit and recharge. I think perhaps the language barrier helped. He had to take what I was saying at its face value, instead of picking up on any nuance. At any rate, he gave his reluctant approval. I was released from all my weekly assignments, for the first time in many, many years.

It was a really odd feeling to have zero responsibilities at the meeting. Not bad, just odd. I could simply sit there. The next meeting randomly happened to conflict with my work schedule, and I missed it. I planned out that over several months I'd reduce my meeting attendance and preaching down to zero, in as inconspicuous a way as possible.

But when it came to actually going to the subsequent meeting, it just felt *so* wonderful that I didn't have to go if I didn't want to. I'm smiling right now remembering. And so I skipped that one, too. And the next. And I never, ever went to another one. My careful plan had gone straight out the window, and it felt marvelous. I had such a sense of lightness. A great weight had been lifted off my soul. It had cost me thirty years of my life, but to experience that feeling of relief was almost—*almost*—worth the price.

"'Give the password,'

said the chief soldier.

'This is my password,'

said the King as he drew his sword.

'The light is dawning,
the lie broken.'"

- The Last Battle

Growth

Taking that step was exhilarating, and simultaneously draining in a way I'd never experienced. It felt like I'd set a new world record at the Olympics, or free soloed Everest. I burned all my matches to get it done, with the result that I had no energy left to change much else in my life right away. Medical staff are a hard-drinking bunch, and I started going out with coworkers sometimes. I had no concept of how to drink socially. Actually, I'm not sure I'd ever set foot in a bar before.

I remember arriving at one gathering where I started by downing a hefty thirty-two-ounce beer in about five minutes. The night continued in that general vein. Later, we packed up to head out. "How are you getting home?" my charge nurse asked, about a foot shorter and ten years younger than me. "Oh, I have my car," I carefully explained. "You're drunk," she said in no uncertain terms.

The thought wobbled its way through my sloshy brain. Drunk? I'd never run into that situation before. Fascinating. It wasn't *quite* as amazing as I'd thought it would be. I'd gone from being quiet and sober to quiet and drunk, instead of the jovial extrovert I'd hoped would emerge. But still it wasn't too bad, all things considered. My accommodating coworkers gave me a ride home. The next morning was less fascination, more aching head.

A couple of years later, I took a vacation by myself to Daytona Beach. I'd heard Jameson whiskey was pretty good, and I bought a bottle. I figured I could get a little buzzed, and then go sit by the beachside pool to enjoy the weather. I drank about five shots and waited a little bit. I didn't notice much difference. Since I didn't want to look like a lush carrying a whiskey bottle around, I had about eight more shots to be safe. Then I went down to the pool.

All thirteen shots hit simultaneously. I have to say I've rarely felt so bad. I couldn't move for fear of throwing up everywhere. I couldn't even see the beach through a spinning blur. Somehow, I made it back up to my room later to experience another first—spending the night drunk on the bathroom floor. I believe that was my first and last time drinking Jameson. I like to think I've been able to moderate my alcohol intake a bit better since then.

The first few years after leaving the JW organization were bewildering. I spent most of the time in a state of shock and depression. I knew leaving had been the right decision. But beyond that, I had no idea what I was doing, or what I should be doing.

I continued working my three shifts each week, but otherwise life was pretty empty. No new friends, nothing to fill the many hours being a JW had consumed each week. I made no attempts to advance in my job, volunteer, or do anything else as far as personal growth. All those things seemed worldly and bad. My body was now free, but my mind was still largely in JW mode.

If I'd explained to my coworkers what was going on, I'm sure I would have found sympathetic ears. But I was ashamed. I was embarrassed I'd been fooled for so many years. I'd been so dense, to have wasted my entire life on this organization.

I thought back to elementary school. The teacher had wanted to put me in the advanced class, but my parents and I had turned it down to make sure my service to Jehovah wasn't hindered. (Whatever that meant for a ten-year-old.) I thought about how I'd left public school and homeschooled for my last six years. How many interesting classes had I missed out on? I played the flute growing up (probably the only talent Terry Crews and I have in common). What if I'd gone to that summer workshop my flute teacher had recommended me for? My life seemed to consist entirely of lost opportunities. I was in my thirties, an RN taking orders from attending physicians younger than I was.

"I'm staring down the road my life has gone Is this where I belong?"

- "Ill Mind of Hopsin 7"
Hopsin

Depression began to creep back in on me. I'd last had a serious spell about eight years earlier, a dark time which somehow, thankfully, seemed to have slowly improved on its own. Back then, I would sit in the darkened lab of the factory where I'd been working as a second-shift security guard. They had many chemicals, one of which was a jar of cyanide. I'd slowly turn the jar in my hand, considering how best to use it without hurting anyone. I'd heard cyanide outgassed from a corpse, so I figured it would be best to use it outside. That way no one else would get hurt. I didn't want to kill myself, necessarily. I just wanted to be not alive anymore. I'm grateful that for whatever reason, I never quite went through with it.

My life felt aimless back then, pointless even, as it again did now. Shortly after that point, I had begun nursing school. I started learning Spanish not much later. My education had given me purpose, and very possibly saved my life. By giving me the tools to objectively assess the lens through which I viewed the world, it had led me to a fierce happiness I'd never known. Paradoxically, it had also seemed to return me back to melancholy and emptiness.

Was education again the answer? I didn't really want to learn another language. I'd chipped away at my nursing degree over the years and had my bachelor's done. My master's was the next logical step. But did I really want to stick with nursing forever? It was, when it came right down to it, a field I got into because it was not wholly disapproved by the JW organization, and because it paid decently—probably not the absolutely best reasons to pursue a career.

"Sometimes

    darkness

      can

  show

     you

         the

       light"

        -"The Light"
           Disturbed

It was somewhere in that low time I found out there was an ex-JW group on Reddit, reddit.com/r/exjw/. I can't remember how I first stumbled on it, but slowly I began reading what people were posting. It was amazing to know so many others had also left the organization. (The subreddit had over fifty thousand members in 2020.) They had the same confusion, anger, bitterness, relief, and depression I was feeling.

Eventually, I started to post my own thoughts and stories. There was a lot of catharsis in bonding over our shared experiences. I loved being able to commiserate about things only other JWs could appreciate. One day someone posted a photo of the exact same custom Bible I'd gotten as a gift for temping at Bethel. The connection gave me a rush of excitement.

I found out there were books written by ex-JWs. First and foremost was *Crisis of Conscience*, by former Governing Body member Raymond Franz. His writing reminded me so much of a *Watchtower* article in its measured cadence and mild tone. It finally helped solidify I'd made the right decision in leaving. The information he could share from working at the highest levels made it clear this was not a unique organization guided by Almighty God. It was just a group of men bumbling along.

I found JWfacts.com. It is a website created by Paul Grundy, a former Bethelite, who laid out all the research he'd done before deciding to leave the organization. It was a wealth of information on virtually every subject having to do with JWs. Who knew the Notorious B.I.G., Ja Rule, Xzibit, Donald Glover, and Patti Smith had all been raised as Jehovah's Witnesses?

I learned of former Ministerial Training School graduate Lloyd Evans' "John Cedars" YouTube channel. Like JWfacts, it also takes a calm, objective look at all things JW. Not that it's important, but all the same I felt better that these three men in particular hadn't just been on the fringes of the JW organization. They were very dedicated, and had progressed further than I had. And still they had drawn the same conclusion: it was not the truth.

I began to learn about the psychological aspects of being in, and then leaving, an organization that exerts such control over its members. It is a form of PTSD, and there was even a specific term for it—religious trauma syndrome. I learned that while my thinking had been molded by a lifetime of religious inculcation, it's also possible to retrain the mind in more positive pathways.

And I found it's actually never too late to start living. You should do what you truly wish to do. The time will pass either way. I began trying to think, not in terms of what I had lost, but in terms of what the possibilities are.

There were physical changes I hadn't anticipated. Like most JWs, I was overweight. What point was there working to get fit? Jehovah would turn my body into perfection in paradise. In the meantime, eating is a great pastime for Witnesses. Every party is a potluck. Every morning spent preaching is punctuated by a visit to the local coffee shop. Almost as fun as the conventions and assemblies is deciding where to eat out afterwards.

But after leaving, I found I lost weight. I tried CrossFit for a year. I got into running and did a couple of marathons. Long walks and bike rides by myself gave me time to sort out my jumbled thoughts. Time spent on local park trails helped me connect with the present-day world in a way I hadn't before. I'd always been so focused on the paradise to come, I hadn't really noticed the natural beauty which already existed.

"If you want to view
paradise

Simply look around
and view it

Anything you want to,
do it

Want to
change the world?

There's
nothing to
it"

- "Pure Imagination"
  Willy Wonka and the Chocolate Factory

Growth

Running on trails, I learned you need to look where you would *like* to go. If you focus on a root or rock, invariably you trip right over it. Better just to put it in your periphery. As *Seinfeld* said about cleavage, "You get a sense of it, then you look away." I started using that philosophy in life. JWs are newshounds. Any disaster, any bad thing that happened—it was proof the end was just around the corner. I was an NPR junkie myself. But I started consciously listening less and less. I ignored the newspaper. Sometimes I'd get to work after a few days off, and everyone was talking about some terrible event which happened somewhere. It would be the first I'd heard about it.

I did my best to focus on where I wanted to go, the clear space between the rocks and roots. I found I could ignore political news for months at a time. Somehow the country kept on running just fine without me. I only watched fun movies. I started reading graphic novels instead of written ones. I guess someone needs to focus on saving the world. But at that point, what I needed was to quit cold turkey. I was detoxing from thirty years of negative focus. It was like the juice cleanse to end all juice cleanses. (Pro tip: don't do juice cleanses.)

Okay kids, now let's visit the TMI zone! I'd always struggled with irritable bowel syndrome (IBS). It wasn't uncommon among JWs. One elder in the congregation kept an emergency pair of underwear in his glove box (half as a joke, half not). Another older Witness only went out preaching with us in his camper, so he'd always have a bathroom handy. But a feisty gut became much less of a problem after I left. (It's not gone completely—I love my dairy products more than I love a calm digestive tract, what can I say.)

Another thing I noticed was that for years, I'd struggled with canker sores. Like clockwork, any stressful situation—a new job, final exams, a move—would guarantee several canker sores showing up in my mouth. I always had a tube of Anbesol in the medicine cabinet. The crazy thing is, I haven't had a single one in the years since leaving Jehovah's Witnesses. I've made major job and living changes, each time waiting for the inevitable sores to make an appearance. But they haven't. It gives me an inkling of just how much stress my body was trying to tamp down as a Witness.

In organizations which exercise such comprehensive control over the lives of members, any sliver of personal autonomy members can find is coveted. For Witnesses, it is especially noticeable among wives of circuit overseers. They have, I think, the hardest job in the entire religion; it is the ultimate convergence of powerlessness and obligation. They must always be on: well-spoken, well-dressed, well-mannered—the gold standard of JW womanhood.

Simultaneously, she has almost zero control over anything. Virtually every week is spent in a different family's home, eating meals prepared by another woman, her year planned out to the hour by a man in a Bethel office far away. Every seven days, she sees a fresh example of a JW wife up close and personal, one who gets to choose things for herself. What bed sheets to sleep on. What toilet paper to use. Whether or not to have children. One who gets to spend Friday nights with her husband, instead of watching him walk out the door every week to attend another in a never-ending series of elders' meetings.

As a result, circuit overseers' wives clutch at any autonomy available, like a drowning person desperately scrabbling for a life preserver. Before a circuit overseer's visit to a congregation, it's rare that the elders don't receive a detailed list of extensive dietary restrictions for meals provided, a list prepared by the circuit overseer's wife. It is a tiny, fledgling effort to carve out a bit of personal agency in a religion which proffers none.

"When wives of circuit overseers **display a quiet and mild spirit, show warmth and love, exhibit a happy countenance,** and **have an uncomplaining spirit,** they win the support and confidence of others. They should **set a fine example for others to follow.** Each circuit overseer should help his wife to **be zealous in field service,** to **give meaningful comments** at congregation meetings, and to **display respect for headship** by **working cooperatively under his direction."**

- Circuit Overseer Guidelines
Chap. 23, par. 2

Vague autoimmune illnesses are widespread among JWs. When chronic fatigue syndrome became widely known in the 1990s, many Witnesses reported having the disorder. Nowadays, any congregation you visit will have a number of women reporting fibromyalgia. In my layman's opinion, two factors probably contribute. One is the general unhealthiness and extra weight many Witnesses have. And the second, perhaps the major contributor, is simply the enormous stress of the Witness life.

Stressful situations…it reminds me of a time we went to a baseball game when I was a kid. One quirk to point out first—JWs don't salute the flag or sing national anthems. It's a way to signal their political neutrality. What this means is that children are required to take a stand almost from the day they start kindergarten. Alone in the classroom, they *must* refuse to do the flag salute. (Random trivia: the U.S. flag salute used to be done with arm outstretched, Nazi-style. Only when Hitler co-opted it did the United States switch to hand-over-heart.)

I recall a day when Susannah, perhaps seven at the time, was crying as she walked out of school to the car where we were waiting. Another time, I came home myself after school on a hot spring day. I was also around seven or eight at the time. I quietly went up to my room, put all the blankets I could find on the bed, and then burrowed underneath them. I was hoping I would die by overheating. (I emerged a little while later—flushed, sweaty, and to my surprise, still very much alive.)

It's really hard to be different as a little kid. And mingled with that, the feeling that each misstep is akin to smearing mud on God's name. I wanted to make him happy. But from what I could understand at the meetings each week, I sensed much room for improvement. I was not one hundred percent good all the time. And in my young brain, that translated to: if I wasn't a flawlessly good person, then I must be a bad person. If I did something wrong, it wasn't that I had made a mistake. I *was* a mistake...

Every baseball game starts with the national anthem, which is an issue for JWs. (Remember, Jehovah is watching. He likes catching a minor-league game now and then as much as the next person.) Witnesses basically do one step less than everyone else in the room when it comes to displays of national pride. If everyone is saluting the flag, you can stand but not salute. If everyone is standing for the national anthem, you stay seated. So, when the national anthem started playing that day we went to a game, like clockwork everyone stood up. And my mom did, too.

It's hard to put into words how much you want to stand with everyone else. The urge is almost irresistible. It's like magnets are pulling you up. But next to her Susannah and I stayed seated, shooting her looks of indignation. For years, we'd put up with disapproving glares and murmurs. (Most Americans see no conflict between being godly and also patriotic.) No way did our mom get to stand up. She had *chosen* to become a Witness, as an adult. She got to skip all the hassle of being a JW kid in school. It was time for her to get a taste. Flustered, she looked at us and sat back down uncertainly. For subsequent games, we employed the time-honored JW tactic of getting to our seats late, after the anthem had been sung.

It isn't an easy way of life, standing out as so different from the rest of society. I wonder sometimes what would happen if the organization changed its stance on shunning. How many would quit, if they weren't in danger of being cut off from family and friends?

Or what if the hope of living forever in paradise wasn't there? Would as many people still follow all the tenets of the Watchtower organization? When eternal life seems to be in your grasp, legends attest that people get crazy. Stories talk about drinking mercury, eating gold, searching endlessly for a fountain of youth. For modern-day Witnesses, it might mean you shun your own family, you let your child die instead of getting a blood transfusion, or you cover up child sexual abuse. The question is, what if there was no dangling carrot of paradise? What if there was no hope of seeing your dead loved ones resurrected back to life?

Would Witnesses stick with it just for its own sake? JWs always say that even if it weren't the true religion, it's still the best way of life. Witnesses posting on Instagram use the hashtag #BestLifeEver. But I wonder. I imagine the Watchtower organization doesn't really want to find out. Hence, the constant flow of paintings and photos in the literature depicting the coming paradise on earth.

The JW conception of paradise is basically Switzerland in the summer, all snow-capped mountains and green meadows. There are also endless supplies of tropical fruit, panda bears, and tame lions. There are beautiful houses, but no electrical wires or telephone poles. It's never really explained where the nails and plumbing fixtures come from. Are there some JWs who have to work in factories in the paradise? Do building supplies appear on the ground each morning, as manna did for the Israelites? The organization leans very heavily on Revelation 20:12 for the answer. They explain vaguely that "new scrolls" opened after Armageddon will clear up all the questions.

"Many have wondered how accidents would be avoided during Christ's kingdom, since we are told that nothing shall then hurt or destroy.

Most accidents are due to gravitation and its effects.

Falling from aeroplanes (including the negative gravity type- the heavier-than-air machines will then be obsolete), etc., may be avoided by an individual negative gravity device."

- Golden Age 03/24/26, p. 404

The other thing I always wondered about is the cleanup after Armageddon. As Lloyd Evans has pointed out in his videos, the JW paradise will be built atop seven billion non-JW dead bodies. How will so many corpses be disposed of? Will some Witnesses have to do it? The literature says carrion birds will do a lot of the work picking the remains clean (although I'm not sure the bones of seven billion skeletons would be any less disturbing).

"Doubtless the Almighty God will use some **highly scientific** means, whether including *antimatter* or not, to dispose of the **surplus of decaying bodies** in a speedy and sanitary way."

- *"The Nations Shall Know That I Am Jehovah"- How?*
p. 377, par. 22

I guess I just tried not to think too much about that part. Instead, I'd think about my dream home—a log cabin near a lake. Many ex-JWs can recall that while preaching, they'd pick out houses they'd like to move into after the current residents die at Armageddon. It's kind of creepy, and I don't remember my friends and I really doing that. But we could appreciate a beautiful house. (In particular, JWs become experts on doors.) Some homes I'd file away in my head, like a girl cutting out pictures from a bridal magazine. The direction from the organization was: make paradise real to yourself. Strengthen your faith. The clearer it was in our mind's eye, the less apt we'd be to stray.

However, this was strictly a mental exercise. There aren't really any attempts by JWs to make the world a better place right now. Why bother? Any day now, Jehovah will start over with a clean slate. Unlike many religions, there is no charity arm that runs soup kitchens, homeless shelters, or detox facilities. The *Awake* magazine often has articles on plants and animals. But rarely is there any emphasis on saving the environment, recycling, alternative energy, global warming, or preserving endangered natural spaces. These issues are raised only inasmuch as they are proof we're living in "the last days."

The funny thing is, a very strong "volunteering" culture exists among JWs. They want to help others. But the only outlet for that desire we got trained on is preaching. It's a little like a kid inculcated from infancy to be a firefighter. His parents are firefighters. He knows how it benefits the community. He sees the personal satisfaction to be gained fighting fires. But each time he goes to the twice-a-week firefighter classes, there is no actual training on putting out fires. Instead, they practice sales techniques to recruit more firefighters.

Growth

I should point out that the Watchtower organization frequently touts its relief work. It will go to cities hit by hurricanes or flooding and rebuild members' houses. Groups of JWs with construction experience volunteer for a week or longer to help in the rebuilding effort (paying their own way). However, what I never realized—because it's never mentioned—is that in exchange, Watchtower expects the homeowners to hand over their insurance checks. Since the labor is donated, the organization only has to pay for construction materials. So there are benefits in two ways: it's good for public relations, and it turns a tidy profit.

As a side benefit, the volunteer workers feel good, like they're making a difference. They prove to themselves this *must* be God's one true religion. So they stick even tighter to Watchtower. Win-win-win. Plus, the organization can use a specific natural disaster to ask for extra donations from JWs. That's more wins than…than that team that wins a lot. What can I say, watching team sports is frowned on by the religion. My sports knowledge has more holes than a Swiss cheese on rye.

Law

Secret. Strong enough for a man, pH balanced for a woman. Why is that commercial burned into my brain? If I remember correctly, I think it was Sherlock Holmes who described his mind as a large desk filled with little drawers. To learn something new, he had to empty a drawer of some other fact to make room for it. I feel like there's a lot more useful info I could retain besides old deodorant jingles, but such is life.

Speaking of secrets, when I became a ministerial servant, sometimes I'd read out letters from headquarters during the announcements. Only at that point did I realize many of the letters had sections for elders' eyes only. Those sections generally gave a more thorough explanation of the issue than the high points I'd read aloud.

In the same vein, elders are issued the rulebook called *Shepherd the Flock of God*. I don't remember ever talking with my dad about it, yet somehow Susannah and I knew we weren't allowed to look in it. Being dutiful non-elders, we never tried to sneak a peek at its almost three hundred pages of rules and instructions.

I never thought about it at the time, but if I was having Bible study sessions with someone interested, there's not really a point before baptism when you sit them down and explain how disfellowshipping or disassociation works, and what the rules are about it all. We kind of left those parts out.

Roughly eighty-five pages of the elder book are dedicated just to judicial proceedings: how to handle it when someone sins. That's a lot of rules. Again, this is information regular congregation members are not allowed to see. Even as a ministerial servant I have to admit ignorance on a lot of it. I was too much of an unadventurous straight arrow to ever get into trouble requiring a judicial committee. So I can't speak from firsthand experience. But thanks to anonymous elders leaking copies of the rulebook, it's not too hard to find out how it all works. And it is fascinating reading.

Let's say I got jiggy with it (is that still an expression?) and had sex before marriage. Perhaps my conscience was squawking, and I confess to an elder. Or maybe someone else found out about it. Like many totalitarian regimes or cults, there's a strong informant culture in the JW religion. (To have those as your bedfellows is a bit concerning, no?) The basic idea is that if it's discovered you knew about something but didn't report it, now *you're* guilty too, of covering up a sin. Plus, don't you want me to get spiritual healing from the elders? What kind of a true friend are you, not telling on me? So stuff usually comes out pretty quickly.

"One day Mary faced a dilemma. In processing medical records she came upon information indicating that a patient, a fellow Christian, had submitted to an abortion. Did she have a scriptural responsibility to expose this information to elders in the congregation, even though it might lead to her losing her job, to her being sued, or to her employer's having legal problems?...

Mary was somewhat apprehensive about the legal aspects, but felt that in this situation Bible principles should carry more weight than the requirement that she protect the privacy of the medical records...

Courage and discretion would be needed."

— *Watchtower* 09/01/87, pp. 12, 14

Two elders will begin an investigation, to see if the sin did occur. They will talk to eyewitnesses. If they have either a confession or a minimum of two eyewitnesses, they'll convene a judicial committee of three elders. JWs adamantly hold that at least two witnesses to the sin are required in order to proceed, if there's not a confession. This gets very sticky when it comes to child abuse.

Generally, a child molester is going to make sure there are *no* witnesses to the abuse. As a result, if a child (one eyewitness) is able to courageously tell an adult they've been abused, but the perpetrator denies it, no judicial committee will be formed. The elders will "leave the matter in Jehovah's hands." Life will continue as before, with the congregation at large unaware. (Except elders, I guess. One of the perks of being an elder—you know who to keep your kids away from.) If the family wants to report the abuse to police, they are not officially punished for doing so. However, there has always been internal pressure not to drag Jehovah's name through the mud by making congregation affairs public.

In a number of states, clergy are mandated reporters of child abuse. That being said, it is surprising to read the instructions in the 2020 edition of the elder handbook. There is no list provided of those states. Nor does it direct elders to a website listing the states with such laws (since laws do change over time). Instead, the directive is to always, always immediately call the Watchtower legal department before doing anything. Those are the same instructions JW elders have been guided by for decades.

Perhaps the organization just doesn't trust elders to know their state's guidelines. But more likely, it's a matter of wanting to control what is revealed to the police. Without that step of calling headquarters first, most elders would probably err on the side of caution (and common sense) and pass on a child's report of abuse to the authorities, even if not strictly required to. It's not as if the police are going to arrest you for being a concerned adult. It's intriguing to contrast the phrasing in the 2020 edition of the elders' rulebook to the 2019 article congregations studied together about child molestation.

"...*immediately*
call the Legal Department
for legal advice
when the elders learn of
an accusation of child abuse."

> - *Shepherd the Flock of God*
> April 2020 ed., Ch. 14, par. 7

"...elders
endeavor
to
comply
with secular laws
about reporting allegations of abuse."

> - *Watchtower* May 2019
> p. 10, par. 13

While the first phrase describes a definite requirement, the second has wiggle room. Why did the Governing Body feel the need to insert the words "endeavor to"? Would elders have difficulty contacting law enforcement? Unless there are elders somewhere that haven't hopped on the newfangled fad of owning a telephone, notifying police is pretty straightforward. (Interestingly, in years prior, the instructions were for an elder to go to a corner pay phone and give an anonymous tip about child abuse to police if need be. Since pay phones have disappeared, those instructions have become a bit impractical, and hence have been deleted.)

Barbara Anderson is a former Bethelite who has spent many years examining how Jehovah's Witnesses handle child molestation. Among the documents she has accumulated is an internal JW form called the "Child Abuse Telememo." It lists the questions the Bethel official taking a report of child abuse would ask. The form has been revised over the years, and notable on one revision is "Survey Question 9":

"How many elders felt that the victim was somewhat at fault or willingly participated in the acts?"

I'm not sure whether that's a question they ask currently. The idea it existed at all for some period of time is disturbing.

As a nurse, each state I've worked in required me to be a mandated child abuse reporter. In fact, hospitals generally always have a social worker on site. It's her job to field reports of child abuse or elder abuse, among other responsibilities.

One time, I received a new patient from the emergency department. She was an elderly woman. Her adult son was there with her, but I was getting a weird vibe from him. When we washed her up, she was covered in bruises in various stages of healing, a classic sign of abuse. It felt really good to report what we'd found. We were glad we could protect her from harm when she was unable to protect herself.

But for a JW, that natural human instinct to protect those weaker is coolly balanced against what is seen as the greater good.

Nicholas Angel:
"You should be
ashamed!
Calling yourself
a community that
cares."

Reverend Shooter:
"Oh,
but we
do
care,
Nicholas."

Joyce Cooper:
"It's *all* about
**the
greater
good."**

NWA members:
[echoing in agreement]
"The
greater
good..."

Nicholas Angel:
"How
can this
be for
*the
greater
good?"*

NWA members:
[echoing]
"The greater good..."

— *Hot Fuzz*

The previously mentioned 2019 *Watchtower* article explains further in paragraph thirteen: "The elders are primarily concerned with maintaining the sanctity of God's name." Jehovah's Witnesses view themselves as God's one true organization on earth. In other words, "God's name" is essentially synonymous with the JW organization. So: is it better to save one person, or an organization?

To use my anecdote about the abused woman, it would be as if her son was a hospital employee. Should her abuse be reported if it would hurt the hospital? After all, the hospital has helped many people. And if the abuse becomes public, some people may avoid that hospital in the future, even though the vast majority of its employees are caring individuals. This has been the dilemma for decades of men leading Jehovah's Witnesses. And as a general rule, the decision always comes down on the side of protecting the organization first.

"We can bide our time,
   we can keep our thoughts in
      our hearts,

deploring maybe
   evils done by the way,

      but approving the high and
      ultimate purpose."

- Saruman to Gandalf
  Lord of the Rings
  "Fellowship of the Ring"

That seems inexplicable, but consider JW beliefs. They believe that any day now, God's heavenly armies will come to wreak fierce vengeance on wrongdoers at Armageddon. Child molesters will die (well, not automatically—technically, if they are truly repentant, their sins will be forgiven). And in the new world to follow, the victims actually won't remember the abuse, according to JW reading of Scripture.

"See, I will create
>   new heavens
>   and a new earth.

 The former things
>   will not be remembered,
>   nor will they come to mind."

>>   -Isaiah 65:17
>>   *New International Version*

"And he will wipe out
>   every tear from their eyes,
>   and death will be no more,

 neither will mourning
>   nor outcry
>   nor pain be anymore.

 The former things have passed away."

>>   - Revelation 21:4

(I do wonder, though—are you still *you*, if vast swaths of your memories and experiences have been wiped away?) And so, from the organization's perspective, are a few years of injustice and pain really so bad, when in exchange Watchtower will guide you to paradise, to an infinity of joy and happiness? To JW leadership, it's a more than fair trade. After all, they point out, the Bible says we "must enter into the Kingdom of God through many tribulations" (Acts 14:22).

For some Witnesses, their tribulation is a chronic illness. For others, it is government persecution. And for some JW children, getting their ticket to paradise means being sexually molested by a fellow Witness whose track record may (unbeknownst to local child protective services) already have generated an overflowing confidential envelope in the Kingdom Hall's file cabinet.

"Thirty-three years of

evil

for an eternity of good!

Who would not willingly pay the price!"

-Golden Age 07/20/1921 p. 615

Of course, if there is no paradise coming, this line of reasoning—morally dubious from the start—crumbles completely. The rule requiring two eyewitnesses in order to take action is discerned even more clearly to be a grave error in judgment—and beyond that, incredibly cruel.

Jesus explained that a loving shepherd would leave his flock of ninety-nine sheep behind to boldly rescue one lost sheep in danger (Luke 15:4). But if one child has been abused, the two-witness rule means many of these little lambs are left to figure out their own rescue, if they can. They may have to continue greeting their abuser twice weekly at congregation meetings. They see the unsuspecting congregation continue to treat the person with love and respect. And they see the shepherds they turned to for help do nothing but twiddle their thumbs. Small wonder many abuse survivors later leave the JW organization. They are unable to reconcile the loving public message with their own coldly inflexible experience.

"We are
    billions
        of
beautiful
            hearts
       and
           you
              sold
                us
             down
         the
            river
                too
                  far"

— "What About Us"
P!nk

Are Jehovah's Witnesses right? The law requiring two witnesses for Israelites in Bible times is found at Deuteronomy 19:15. Should it guide elders today in handling crimes of child sexual abuse? Actually, the elder handbook devotes several pages to discussing circumstantial evidence. In particular, it addresses when two JWs have staked out a house to see if a husband is having an affair.

I hadn't realized this was such a common practice that it would be addressed in the handbook. But it makes sense when you consider the JW stance on divorce. Adultery is the only accepted grounds for divorce. If a divorce is for some other reason, say irreconcilable differences, the couple is considered still biblically married by the elders. For example, suppose a husband divorced his wife. The ex-wife isn't allowed by the elders to remarry until the ex-husband is proved to be having sex with someone else—i.e., cheating on his now-imaginary wife.

It all sounds a bit ludicrous as I'm writing it. Nevertheless, it evidently results in a fair number of JW women staking out their ex (along with a second eyewitness in the car, of course). They want to see if he spends an entire uninterrupted night with a woman. Because presumably in that scenario, the two aren't just playing checkers together. This type of juicy circumstantial evidence is sufficient to open a judicial committee on the guy, so an ex-wife who wants to remarry can get on with her life.

Hence, even current JW rules allow for commencing judicial action when a sin wasn't observed by four eyeballs in the room. But even more persuasive is that teaching of Jesus about when an animal falls down a pit on the Sabbath. It's the principle called "pikuach nefesh."

Nothing considered work was to be done that day, on pain of death. God makes it very clear in the Bible. In one biblical narrative, a man was found collecting some firewood on the Sabbath. Jehovah instructs the Israelites to throw stones at the man until he falls down, and then continue until he dies of massive blunt force trauma (Numbers 15:35). However, the Gospels describe Jesus teaching a more nuanced understanding of his Father's command.

"If you have one sheep
  and that sheep falls into a pit

            on the Sabbath,

      is there
      a man among you
      who will not grab hold of it

          and lift it out?

How
    much   more   valuable

                is a man
            than a sheep!"

- Matthew 12:11,12

As with blood transfusions, biblical laws laid down by God himself can be ignored to ease the suffering of another human. (And if a person thinks Jesus Christ was wrong here, it would seem that at that point, by definition, one has ceased to be a Christian.)

The question arises: when JW leadership insists on inflexibly following rules at the expense of hurt children, what have they become? Are they like Jesus? Or are they more like his enemies, the Jewish religious leaders called the Pharisees? The Pharisees were big on rigidly following rules, even minor rules about tithing almost insignificant amounts of herbs. They were somewhat less concerned with godly qualities.

"Woe to you,
  scribes and Pharisees,
    hypocrites!

because you give the tenth of

    the mint
    and the dill
    and the cumin,

      but
        you have disregarded

the weightier matters
    of the Law,
    namely,

      justice
      and mercy
      and faithfulness.

    These things
      it was
    necessary
        to do,

    yet

not to disregard
the other things."

        - Matthew 23:23

Actually, I guess there is one rule elders could follow. If they find out about child abuse, call the police right away. Every time. Let them handle it. If watching a million episodes of *Law & Order: SVU* has taught me anything, it's that there are detectives dedicated to investigating these vicious felonies. They're members of an elite squad. *DUN DUN*

Okay, rant over. Let's circle back to judicial committees. So a couple of elders investigated, found that a sin has occurred, and form a judicial committee of three elders. There's something I see now—a judicial committee's purpose is not to find out innocence or guilt. If the committee has formed, the Witness is guilty. The committee's purpose is to determine the degree of punishment. It's based on whether the accused is repentant or not. There are three options for punishment. It's much like the way Starbucks offers three overpriced coffee sizes.

First, you have your private reproof. That's the small coffee (or tall, in Starbucks land). The nice thing is, nothing is announced to the congregation if you're privately reproved. Sure, you'll get counseled. You'll lose "privileges." Privileges are rather like imaginary Internet points. Within one's little sphere, people are quite impressed by them. They signify a lot of time and work invested. But they're completely meaningless in the world at large.

For me as a male, there were a lot of privileges I could get. After baptism, I could start with being able to handle the microphones and sound system. Adjusting the microphones on stage. Taking attendance. Becoming a ministerial servant. An auxiliary pioneer. A regular pioneer. Giving longer and longer talks. Handling the congregation accounting. Being an elder. Talks at circuit assemblies and conventions. Joining the Governing Body. There is literally no end of privileges you can level up to as a guy.

But I regret to inform female readers that having two X chromosomes means far fewer levels available to you. Sorry about that, better luck next time. Your available privileges are mostly all about spending more and more time preaching. I suppose the one other option for women is to get married. Then they can sort of level up as their husbands do.

Being privately reproved will mean losing a lot of privileges. You might even get all the way back down to square one, which is not being allowed to comment during question-and-answer parts of the meeting. And even a three-year-old sitting on her mom's lap can giggle out a "Jehovah" or "Jesus" comment. So it's a humbling thing. Ultimately, I guess that's the point—to humble (should the word be humble or humiliate?) the person and get them to fall back in line.

Next up, the grande coffee: being *publicly* reproved. It includes everything from private reproof. Then it adds being announced during one of the meetings. "So-and-so has been reproved." The shame factor is ramped up a notch, because now everyone knows you've been naughty.

The specific sin isn't announced anymore, like it was in the early years. However, as in most closed groups, the gossip circuit is very big among JWs. Within days, the whole congregation will know everything. What you did, who you did it with, and any other salacious details. The loss of privileges will last maybe a year. If you keep your nose clean, you'll probably be fully restored to good standing by that point.

Option three, the venti coffee, is disfellowshipping. It's the big guns. If you're disfellowshipped, you'll be announced. "So-and-so is no longer one of Jehovah's Witnesses." You're still allowed to enter the Kingdom Hall and attend meetings, but that's it. Nobody is permitted to talk to you. You will be a ghost in the hall. No one will make eye contact or acknowledge your existence.

If you're a minor living at home, your parents will hopefully more or less treat you as before. They'll stop discussing religious matters. The odds seem to run about fifty-fifty on whether or not they'll kick you out of the house. If you've already left home, your family will probably ghost you. JW video presentations show step-by-step how parents should ignore texts, phone calls, and generally any contact from a disfellowshipped child.

In Scientology, this process is called Disconnection. I think that's an apt descriptor. If family members persist in rebelliously keeping up contact, they will most likely lose all *their* privileges. But it will end there. However, if it's not a relative, you can be disfellowshipped yourself for talking to a disfellowshipped person.

"But, even so, are you *really* a friend of God while treating your **brother** as someone to be shunned?

...It would indeed be *better* to 'have intense love for one another,' for 'love covers a multitude of sins.'"

- *Watchtower* 02/15/76, p. 117, par. 13-14

Generally, it will be at least one year before someone disfellowshipped can be "reinstated." At that point, people are allowed to talk to them again. After the announcement that So-and-so has been reinstated, it's like a light switch is flipped. Everyone will come up to the person, smiling, talking, pretending the past year of ostracism never happened.

Steven Hassan's book *Combating Cult Mind Control* reviews a list of questions to ask a member before joining any organization. One is, "Does your group impose restrictions on communicating with former members?" The book explains, "Any legitimate organization would never discourage contact with former members."

I've thought about that a lot. It's definitely true that ignoring your children is not a natural human instinct. The JW organization finds it necessary to regularly reiterate the importance of supporting the disfellowshipping, or shunning, arrangement. It seems to be a recurring topic every year or so. (The word shun appears to have replaced disfellowship in modern society outside of Jehovah's Witnesses.)

Watchtower articles explain that when you shun your children, that's actually the loving thing to do (although the average person would think it's just the opposite). If you truly love your child and want them to live forever in paradise, it's okay to hurt them. Now I know that sounds like what a child abuser would say, but umm…somehow it makes sense when you're a JW.

So those are the three possible outcomes of the judicial meeting. (Again, being found innocent is not really an option.) How do the elders decide which is the right punishment? It depends on whether you're repentant or not. Of course, as JWs say, only Jehovah can read hearts. And he is surprisingly quiet these days about what he knows. So, the elders have to make a judgment call about repentance. It's based on what they see and hear. The elder handbook devotes several pages to teaching the technique, like a book for young magicians explaining step-by-step how to do tricks.

It seems to boil down to two main things, the first being your attitude. Are you genuinely sad about what you've done? (But it advises elders that crying a lot doesn't automatically mean you're sorry. They saw that gambit coming.) Have you apologized to those you've wronged? Did you confess, or did someone have to turn you in? And second, what's your track record? Was it a one-time slip? Have you been hooking up secretly for a year?

There's a distressing number of rather creepy posts on the Reddit ex-JW forum. They are posts in which female redditors talk about their judicial committee hearings. (Men don't seem to run into this particular issue.) They report that the questions seemed to get way more nitty-gritty than would appear necessary, if you've already confessed. Was the sex oral, anal, or vaginal? What positions were you in? How long did it last? Did he orgasm? Did you? Did he insert his fingers? How many? Did you shave? What did your underwear look like? What color was it? The women, many still teenagers, would get uncomfortable giving that much detail to three random men. The elders would explain that being completely forthcoming and cooperative is a positive sign of repentance.

"There were strong erotic and misogynistic elements, as might be expected in a

sexually repressed, male-dominated society

with inquisitors drawn from the class of nominally celibate priests...

'Devil's marks' were found 'generally on the breasts or private parts' according to Ludovico Sinistrari's 1700 book.

As a result, pubic hair was shaved, and the

genitalia were carefully inspected by the exclusively male inquisitors."

- *The Demon-Haunted World*, p. 261
regarding hunting witches in the Middle Ages

So after that, the three elders send the accused out of the room, and discuss and pray about it. Ideally, they come to a unanimous decision. If not, the one dissenter will support the majority vote. They call the person back in and inform him of their decision. There are seven days to appeal if desired. If that happens, a different committee of three will be formed to review the case. From what I gather, the initial decision is almost never overturned. Either way, after the appeal period has passed, the congregation announcement will be made (unless the decision was for private reproof).

The whole process unfortunately seems to be a pretty straightforward example of a Star Chamber trial. There are scores of rules only the elders conducting the committee know about. It is always arranged three-on-one. The accused isn't allowed to see any of the evidence beforehand. You can't bring counsel to advise you. (Actually, if someone says they will bring a lawyer, the process is immediately suspended indefinitely. Pro tip for anyone facing a judicial committee.)

There are quirky things which have been codified over the years. For example, if a wife is on trial, the husband will generally be present. On the other hand, if a husband is on trial, the wife will be present only if he wants her to be. If the husband had an affair, the elders will not give the wife any details they learn. They will simply tell her she is now free to pursue a scriptural divorce if she wishes. (But if she wants to do that, she has to make sure not to have sex with him again before the divorce. The officially-sanctioned JW signal you've forgiven your no-good cheating spouse is having sex.)

If it's a minor living at home, the parents should be present. (As if giving a play-by-play of your sex life to three older guys you know isn't awkward enough, have your parents in the room!)

Some persons on trial develop suicidal ideation. They are on the cusp of losing perhaps the only community they've ever known. As always, the organization has directions. It advises suspending the hearing for the night. The judicial committee should resume the meeting in the next day or so, and share comforting scriptures. In particular, one encouraging verse the rulebook suggests is Hebrews 12:6: "[F]or those whom Jehovah loves he disciplines, in fact, he scourges everyone whom he receives as a son."

"*The Journal of the American Medical Association* describes the Roman practice of scourging:

> 'The usual instrument was a short whip (flagrum or flagellum) with several single or braided leather thongs of variable lengths, in which small iron balls or sharp pieces of sheep bones were tied at intervals...
>
> As the Roman soldiers repeatedly struck the victim's back with full force, the iron balls would cause deep contusions, and the leather thongs and sheep bones would cut into the skin and subcutaneous tissues.
>
> Then, as the flogging continued, the lacerations would tear into the underlying skeletal muscles and produce
>
> quivering ribbons of bleeding flesh.'"

– *Watchtower* 01/01/91, p. 9

The handbook instructs elders to create a detailed signed paper trail of when they met, noting which scriptures and articles they used. That way, they can show they did something if the accused dies by suicide. (Have to watch out for those civil suits.) But, it warns, "The judicial committee should avoid unnecessarily prolonging the case" (Chap. 15, par. 17).

I thought perhaps it would recommend a suicide hotline. Maybe taking the person to the emergency department for an evaluation. But since the elders and the judicial tribunal are themselves the cause of the suicidal thoughts, I guess it doesn't really make sense to simultaneously give advice on tempering the effects of said tribunal. As 2 Corinthians 7:9–10 explains, the entire point of subjecting someone to a judicial committee is to induce potent sadness. Sometimes a committee overshoots sadness and goes right to suicidal ideation. But for the organization, some deaths by suicide here and there are just the cost of doing business. Dropping the judicial committee? Not an option. Rules, you know.

The thing is that, generally speaking, JWs feel like they deserve to receive this discipline. They're not going to get a lawyer. This is understood to be Jehovah God's approved process. It's set up by Jehovah's organization. It's directed by holy spirit. The sinner has created the judicial committee by his wicked actions and needs to be cleansed. JWs believe in the principle of purification by fire. Not literally, but figuratively.

"I will **smelt** away your **dross** as with **lye,** and I *will* remove all your **impurities."**

- Isaiah 1:25

Probably that verse is easier to understand if you happen to run a silver smelter. I'm guessing that's not a job listed in the Occupational Outlook Handbook anymore. Smelting is when you heat up a metal until it's liquid. The impurities come to the surface, and you can skim them away. The impurities are called dross. JWs teach that, on an organizational level, they needed smelting after World War I.

That was a low point in their history. Numbers were stagnant. Their president and board of directors were in prison. They needed to be purified. The dross was brought to the surface and skimmed away. They stopped celebrating birthdays and Christmas. They quit using the cross. All these were practices they found to have "pagan" roots. They strove to grow closer to "the form of worship that is clean and undefiled from the standpoint of our God and Father" (James 1:27). Once cleansed by fire, they were acceptable to Jehovah.

In fact, they explain proudly, they were definitively selected in 1919 as God's one true religion. Other faiths may not have realized they were participating in a global competition. It was apparently like *American Idol*, but for religions. The grand prize was being God's earthly representatives. According to JW canon, everyone else lost in the semifinals. But evidently most religions are sore losers. They have soldiered on like contestants who won't leave the stage, refusing to acknowledge the victory and close up shop.

If Jehovah God's handpicked organization could itself need refining, clearly its individual members could as well. This fits in well with the concept of original sin. It's said we are all fallen from the perfection God created in the Garden of Eden. We need to be cleansed. To be disciplined. We need to be punished. Okay, it's getting a little weird how much this sounds like something from *Fifty Shades of Grey*. But hopefully it helps clarify (ha, smelting pun) why

JWs dutifully submit to judicial committees. That, and the great dread of being cut off from family and community. Also, the whole dying at Armageddon thing.

My dad has long been an elder. Growing up, we had congregation meetings three days each week (down to two now). After almost every meeting, there would be a "brief" impromptu elders' meeting. The phrase is always said with a rueful smile and eye roll among elders' families. A brief elders' meeting lasting less than half an hour was almost unheard of. Many nights we'd be waiting in the hall until 10:30 pm (these were midweek meetings, hence school nights). And frequently, my dad would be gone at least one extra night each week for another elders meeting.

As a kid, I never begrudged him the time. I knew it must take a lot of hours to run the congregation. What I only now realize is the vast majority of those meetings must have been concerned with judicial proceedings. Compiling evidence, interviewing witnesses, passing judgment, and then follow-up meetings in subsequent months with the convicted parties. Elders check in to see if the person is doing everything asked of them. Only then do they gradually lift restrictions and permit a full standing in the congregation once more.

So what to say about all of this? It bums me out that elders have spent so many millions of man-hours on judicial committees over the years. Imagine how lovely it would be if they had instead been playground-building committees, or homeless shelter committees. It grieves me to consider how many Witnesses have had to submit to this ordeal. I'm sure there are a few elders out there who get their jollies from wielding power over the accused person, but I think many more genuinely care about the congregation. They have been trained to think they're sincerely helping the sinner by participating in this.

The striking thing is that for the first seventy years of the JW organization—almost half its existence—it got along just fine without the current style of disfellowshipping. In the beginning, the congregation would meet with the sinner as a group. They would openly discuss his actions with him, and see what could be done. Sometimes he would be unwilling to change. So they would pause their former level of spiritual fellowship. He was downgraded to a person that had never been a member.

"...in the meantime the brother may merely be treated in the **kindly, courteous way** in which it would be *proper for us* to treat any publican or Gentile".

- *Watchtower* 03/01/1919, p. 69

A 1947 *Awake* article harshly criticized the Catholic Church's practice of excommunication (*Awake* 01/08/47, p. 27). But by 1950, the organization had set up the almost identical practice of disfellowshipping as we know it today. A new category of treatment was prescribed. The sinner would be downgraded *below* a non-member. No more would they be treated in a kindly, courteous way. A 1952 *Watchtower* article had rather different instructions.

"Those who are acquainted with the situation in the congregation should **never** say Hello or Goodbye to him. He is not welcome in our midst, we avoid him...

He might put his report in the report box, but we **tear it up** and we **throw it away...**

He should go back to the wicked group that he once came from and **die** with that wicked group with Satan's organization."

- *Watchtower* 03/01/52, p. 141, par. 14-15; p. 133, par. 8

What makes these strong words so uncomfortable to me is that the Society encourages children to get baptized quite young. I was twelve when I took the plunge. I'd say nine to fifteen is the common age range. The thing is, at that ripe old age I wasn't weighing the pros and cons of it. The elders' handbook with its three hundred pages of rules wasn't shown to me, to see if I'd be comfortable with everything. Getting baptized was simply the next expected step for me as a good JW.

Informed consent isn't really a thing JWs do. I witnessed surgical consents a thousand times at the hospital. The physician (usually the intern got stuck with the job, as the new guy) rushes into the patient's room and explains the plan. Then he rattles off a laundry list of what could go wrong. Death, amputation, impotence, hair loss, nose falling off, talking like Mickey Mouse. Whatever he feels like throwing in that day. Three pagers are going off simultaneously on the waistband of his sagging scrubs. Pens out, paper signed. Easy peasy. But not for Jehovah's Witnesses.

When I watched *Going Clear*, the documentary about Scientology, I laughed when it showed a photo of the billion-year contract they sign. How could anyone be so gullible? In the next moment, I was abashed. I realized I had signed up for no less binding a commitment as a twelve-year-old. (Actually, I started at eleven. Before approval for my baptism, I—like all candidates—had three hours of open-book oral exams on JW teachings (since reduced to two hours). I got a little unnerved after the first two sessions, and waited another year before going through with it.)

It's difficult to reconcile the harsh words the JW organization has for those expelled from the group—"He should go back to the wicked group that he once came from and die"—when you think about how many—probably most—joined up as children. They have been raised to believe from infancy. What group does it want them to go to? Are they really hardened sinners who need to be shunned? Or did they slip up by JW standards, and should be welcomed back with open arms when they admit it? After all, in Jesus' story of the prodigal son, there was no tribunal, no punishment, no shunning.

"Many persons are the product of
a religious organization that
took them in hand at
infancy,

shielded them carefully from
any teaching other than
its own,

and prescribed exactly what they
must believe."

- *Watchtower* 06/15/70, p. 357

Well, I've prattled on long enough. I won't go into the circuit overseer handbook which is unseen by elders, or the branch committee handbook which is unseen by circuit overseers. Many, many layers of confidentiality exist in the JW organization. Information is doled out on a need-to-know basis.

It's funny how Jesus could distill the law code given to Moses, which takes up entire books of the Bible, into two rules: Love God, and, Love your neighbor as yourself. But JW leadership has found their adherents to be a lively bunch. Following those two rules hasn't resulted in the level of control the Governing Body evidently hopes for.

And so we're where we're at today, with a myriad of laws both known and secret to keep the organization humming along. If I'm honest, I'm not such a big fan of Secret. I'm more of a Degree Cool Rush man myself.

Intuition

I WAS THINKING ABOUT THE WHOLE NURSING THING TODAY. NOT breastfeeding, although I'm all for that, too. But being a registered nurse. One thing nurses talk about (other than what snacks are in the break room) is learning to trust your gut instinct, your nurse's intuition.

The idea is that as your experience grows, eventually you'll sense when a patient is taking a turn for the worse. You'll feel it before it's really reflected on the monitor. Nurses maybe hype it up a little bit, but I do think it's a real thing. It comes from having seen a certain situation play out a hundred times before.

I've always been frustrated that, while not entirely hopeless as a nurse, I've never had an iota of this magical sixth sense. Sometimes I'd try to make an educated guess. A while back, I had a patient go into a funky heart rhythm right after he got out of surgery (second degree, type-two for those keeping score). It's a rhythm which can shift into a complete heart block. That would mean your heart is beating only about twenty times per minute, requiring an immediate pacemaker to survive.

I was so proud I'd picked up on this, and I rushed out to tell the doctor. He briefly looked up from his charting and just said, "Oh." He ordered an EKG, to get a picture of the heart's electrical activity. It was the end of my shift, and I left before seeing how it shook out.

I snagged the overnight nurse the next morning to ask what happened. As it turned out, absolutely nothing. His heart had simply corrected its own rhythm during the night. I was glad for the patient, but I was so bummed with my stupid nurse's intuition (or lack thereof). It never zeroed in on the right thing.

Now it may well be that my DNA just lacks the special sauce for having this sixth sense. But on the other hand, I'm pretty sure it may have atrophied from my many years as a JW. In the Watchtower organization, there's no room for thinking for yourself. You shouldn't try connecting the dots on your own.

A while back, I was watching video of the 2018 JW Annual Meeting. Whenever the camera would pan out to the audience, you could see they were on tenterhooks, as one speaker after another left cliffhangers about which country today is the King of the North from Bible prophecy (not to be confused with the King *in* the North from *Game of Thrones*). The listeners had no idea what the answer would be, and they weren't trying to figure it out. They just waited eagerly for someone to tell them what to think.

Listening to your gut is a big no-no in JW land. It's probably because there are plenty of things that raise red flags if you don't push them way down.

"Any idea is a good one, except the *not happy* ones. Those you push down deep inside where you'll never, ever, ever, EVER find them."

- Princess Unikitty
The LEGO Movie

But take courage, me hearties! All hope is not lost. The merest glimmer of the thought that possibly JWs aren't all they're cracked up to be is proof that sixth sense still lives, even if it's buried 20,000 leagues under the sea. It's probably very, very quiet at first. It's gotten a bit flabby and out of shape.

But if you can show it just a bit of love, a little bit of attention, you can follow your gut to what you *know* deep down is true. Even if nothing is showing up just yet on the monitor to everyone else around you. To co-opt the popular JW phrase, you can make the truth your own.

It's a little scary, the thought of not having someone there to tell you what to do next, what to think—to tell you who you are. Scary but exciting. It's like when your pants are filled with Jello: weird at first, but eventually it gets pretty comfortable. That little intuitive voice inside has space to get louder, more strident. It can get buff. We can find out who we are, and what we think about things. Probably it will take a lifetime. Even then, we might not figure it all out. That's okay. Peter Pan said it well.

"To live...to live will be an awfully big adventure."

— *Hook*

Death

Linda was one of my preceptors when I first started working after graduating nursing school. A new RN's preceptor is a kind of a big deal. They're your mentor, the person who will hopefully transform you from scared new grad into someone with a mildly decent grasp of what you're doing. They can shape the rest of your career by how they teach you those first twelve weeks or so.

Both my preceptors were women who'd been nurses for many years. They had a wealth of experience to share. But outside forces conspired against us. Partway through my initial weeks, my first preceptor's husband died, still a young man. She was heartbroken, and I completely understood when she asked our boss if someone else could take over precepting me. A good mentor wants to be able to give one hundred percent. So I moved on to my second preceptor.

Nurses are wont to say that you learn more the first year on the job than in all of nursing school, and I was indeed learning a tremendous amount. And then it happened. My second preceptor's husband died out of the blue. What was happening? Was it me? Was I a Jonah, visiting disaster on each preceptor one by one? I don't think anyone took that too seriously. All the same, my boss decided it was high time to wrap up my orientation, and decreed me ready to strike out on my own. I quite agreed—no point tempting fate a third time.

I think the best way to sum up how JWs deal with death is: it's complicated. The doctrine says there is no soul that survives death. When you die, you are completely, one thousand percent dead. It's usually likened to being asleep, unconscious of time passing. (Which, while a useful analogy for adult JWs, becomes problematic for younger kids. Developmentally, they are thinking in very literal terms, and get death and sleep jumbled up together.) Essentially, JWs believe all good people are stored in God's memory, like little video clips. And after Armageddon, a grand resurrection will begin on earth.

Watchtower writers have given the resurrection a lot of thought over the years. For example, what if you unfortunately went through a woodchipper at your demise, *Fargo*-style? Well, the answer is people don't get the same body when they're resurrected. It's along the lines of the book or show *Altered Carbon*. God downloads your consciousness into a new (hopefully Adonis-like) body. That's why Jesus' disciples didn't recognize him when he appeared after his resurrection. He was picking different bodies each time. Were any of them a redhead, I wonder? Just to mix it up.

So does everyone get resurrected at once, like the wildest family reunion ever? The Bible is silent on the matter, but again the organization has it all figured out. They use a starting figure of six million people surviving Armageddon.

"Then if, after allowing, say, **100 years** spent in their training and in 'subduing' a portion of the earth (Ge 1:28), God purposes to bring back **three percent** of this number, this would mean that each newly arrived person would be looked after by **33** trained ones. Since a yearly increase of **three percent, compounded, doubles** the number about every **24 years,** the entire **20 billion (20,000,000,000)** could be resurrected before **400 years** of Christ's **Thousand Year** Reign had elapsed".
- *Insight on the Scriptures* Vol. 2, p. 793

It goes in reverse chronological order. I welcome back my grandparents, get them settled, and then they welcome back *their* grandparents, and so on until the very last guy, Abel of Cain-and-Abel fame. (The doctrine has gone back and forth over the years, but currently JWs teach there will be no resurrection for Adam and Eve. They had their shot.) However, the organization figures Bible bigwigs like Moses and Abraham will be resurrected right off the bat to help run things. Ergo, Rutherford's ten-bedroom house in San Diego. (I'm not quite sure how they would have gotten to California from the Middle East. One of those negative-gravity airplanes, perhaps.)

One thing that's always bugged JWs is whether you're still married when you're resurrected. What happens if a widow remarried, and now both husbands show up simultaneously for tea and crumpets? Which guy does she live with? The organization has never been shy about telling JWs the answer. However, what answer you got depended on the era you were a Witness.

Will Resurrected People Still Be Married?

NO- *Golden Age* 04/02/30, p. 445
YES- *"The Truth Shall Make You Free"* (1943) pp. 362-4
NO- *Watchtower* 10/15/50, p. 381
YES- *Watchtower* 09/15/54, p. 575
NO- *Watchtower* 11/15/61, p. 703
NO- *Watchtower* 10/15/67, p. 638
NO- *Watchtower* 06/01/87, pp. 30-31
MAYBE- *Watchtower* 12/15/13, p. 29
MAYBE- *Watchtower* 08/15/14, pp. 29-30

The answer over the years has been less a dimmer switch sliding to full brightness and clarity, and more someone randomly flicking the switch on and off. As a result, some Witnesses stay single just to hedge their bets. One elder in my congregation lost his wife in a car accident. They were an absolutely beautiful family. In subsequent years, there were dozens of women ready to marry him at the drop of a hat, but he steadfastly never remarried. He is awaiting the time he and his wife will be reunited in paradise.

With such a strong resurrection hope, death for JWs is complex. On the one hand, you're devastated about the loss. On the other hand, you're glad the person died this side of Armageddon. JWs explain that even some Witnesses will probably be executed at Armageddon, since their heart wasn't truly in it. But death right now means they've guaranteed themselves a resurrection for sure. It's better than holding a winning lottery ticket, if Witnesses played the lottery, which they don't because hello, gambling.

Jehovah's Witness funerals are fairly traditional for the most part. There are often the typical visiting hours at a funeral home, and then a Bible talk the next morning at the Kingdom Hall, followed by the burial. It's important for family not to grieve too much. They are allowed a few quiet tears. However, a lot of crying makes other JWs start to get suspicious. Where is their faith? Don't they really believe in the resurrection?

Death isn't uncommon in the ICU. I'd get uncomfortable at times, seeing some families openly wail and beat their chests in grief. Used to the restrained and slightly uptight JW funerals, it struck me as wrong to carry on so much. I would have to reprimand myself to be more culturally sensitive. I needed to be more open to ways other people do things.

"Nevertheless, while we as Christians certainly do grieve because of death,

we do not sorrow

'as the rest also do **who have no hope.'**

(1 Thessalonians 4:13)

We do not indulge in **unreasonable extremes** of grieving because

we are not **confused** as to the condition of the dead."

— *Awake* 07/08/01, p. 13

Death

One time an elder died in our congregation. He was young. It was a brain tumor. His son was deemed too little to go to the funeral, and I was assigned to hang out with him at my house while the funeral was going on. I was maybe thirteen, and Andy was a few years younger than me. I didn't know how to handle the whole situation. It was one of the first times each of us had had to face death, and neither of us really knew what to say or do. We definitely didn't want to bring up why we were together that morning.

My house had no video games or cable TV. I kept glancing at the kitchen clock as it ticked away in the silence, willing time to go faster until his family would pick him up and the awkwardness could end. Casting about for something to do, I finally suggested we could go for a walk in the woods surrounding my backyard. Neither one of us really wanted to go back to the still house, and we wandered further than I'd been before. Eventually we came to a small clearing in the trees. It was an old forgotten cemetery.

Weathered tombstones stood at crazy angles, their formerly smooth white surfaces turned rough and mottled. The inscriptions had been worn down by decades of winter storms. You could hardly read the names and dates anymore. My heart sank. The whole goal for the morning had been to studiously avoid the subject of death. Andy didn't say anything. He slowly walked through the long grass, looking at the old grave markers.

"My dad died," he said quietly, not looking at me.

"Yeah," I replied. "I know."

I had nothing else to offer. Maybe I should have talked about the resurrection, about how he'd see his dad again soon. But in the moment, that seemed hollow to me. It was something you'd tell a stranger you met out preaching. No platitudes could correct the unfairness of losing your dad so young. The resurrection was for an unknown future version of ourselves. On that morning, we possessed only loss.

JW funeral discourses aren't quite like other funerals. The elder will take a couple of minutes to talk about the life of the deceased. But most of the thirty minutes will be taken up by explaining the resurrection. He'll talk about what we have to do to make sure we're there when the person comes back. If you were feeling cynical, you could describe it as a recruitment pitch to join Jehovah's Witnesses, directed at friends and relatives in attendance who aren't yet members.

In movie funerals I saw, people would get up to share their memories of the person. That was completely foreign to me. One time an older JW died. Her particular funeral was held at the funeral home itself. Her granddaughter wasn't a Witness, and during the funeral she got up to give a little eulogy. I can't recall now whether she spoke or read a poem. Maybe she sang a song her grandma had liked. I just remember I'd never seen anything like that done before. I had no feelings of it being a good or bad thing, just blankness. I didn't know what to think, because no one had told me what to think about it.

When my grandma on my dad's side died, I'd stopped being a Witness a couple of years earlier. It was a traditional Catholic funeral. My cousins and I were the pallbearers. Many, many years had passed since I'd been in a Catholic church. I meant to walk in with an anthropological flair. I would be an observer, curious about the customs of a secluded Amazonian tribe. Instead, I could feel the vestiges of my JW indoctrination still hanging around just beneath the surface, like algae in a pool that needs vacuuming. I felt my lip curl subtly at the trappings of "false religion"—the high ceilings, the stained glass, the long robes of the priest, the incense.

I was nervous about the communion part. I had to participate in the ceremony as a pallbearer. But I just didn't think I could bring myself to take the wafer and wine. Reading my mind, the priest said if we didn't wish to take communion, we could just cross our arms when we came forward. Sitting in the front row with the other pallbearers, I could feel my parents' eyes boring into my back. They were pondering what I would do when I got up, I who had abandoned my childhood faith. How far had I fallen, they wondered, praying silently it wasn't *that* far.

I stood and took my place in line. My cheeks burned a bit as we shuffled forward toward the priest. When I came to the front, I stiffly jerked my arms into an X across my chest and turned back to my seat. I knew my mom and dad had sunk back into their pew, relief washing over them. There is still hope, they probably thought, there is always hope.

Glinda:

"Elphie, listen to me, just say you're sorry!
    You can still be with the wizard
    What you've worked and waited for
    You can have all you ever wanted

Elphaba:
    I know

      but

    I don't want it
    No, I can't want it

        anymore

Something has changed within me
something is not the same

I'm through with playing by
the rules of

someone else's game"

      - "Defying Gravity"
        Wicked

Death

A couple of years later, my grandma on my mom's side died. We all returned to Rochester, New York, the city where my parents had converted to Jehovah's Witnesses. Unlike my other grandma, who had five kids and dozens of grandkids and great-grandkids, this was a small gathering. There was just my mom and her sister, four of us grandkids, and several great-grandkids. My grandma had outlived almost all of her friends. The visiting hours passed slowly, punctuated by the occasional Witness coming to say hi to my parents.

After a while, my dad stood up. He directed us all into two rows of seats, and began giving a traditional JW funeral talk. He explained how she would be coming back to live in a paradise on earth, and how we needed to be Jehovah's Witnesses to see her again.

I was caught off guard as a tiny flame of anger lit up in me. I knew my grandma believed in going to heaven. She hadn't been a hardcore churchgoer, but generally when she went, it was to an Eastern Orthodox or Catholic church. This was her funeral, her day. Why did my dad think his beliefs took precedence over hers? I smiled inside, imagining what would happen if a priest stood up to preach a sermon at *his* funeral, explaining that, well actually, he was up in heaven right now watching over all of us.

My emotion surprised me. It was like a friendly dog who suddenly chomps on your leg. I couldn't really see my dad pulling a stunt like that at his own mother's funeral. His three brothers would have picked him up like a long two-by-four and carried him off the stage—three bald, middle-aged, mustachioed bouncers in perfect sync.

I scooched to the edge of my seat and prepared to walk out in protest, when I glanced over to my aunt and her family. They were solid nondenominational Christians, active in their church. My cousin had made several mission trips to foreign countries. They sat quietly as my dad blathered on, giving the exact same talk for his mother-in-law that he would give for a perfect stranger. And I realized if they could do it, so could I. I could love my grandma by not leaving her alone while JW doctrine wafted over her casket like chlorine gas over a World War I trench.

Afterward, my aunt graciously walked over and thanked my dad for the effort. When I asked my mom later, she told me grandma had said she wanted him to say something at her funeral. Whether that is true, and whether a JW funeral talk is what she meant, I can't say.

The next day, my cousin gave a eulogy. She described how grandma had let her move in when my cousin was struggling for a while. I never knew that. I realized there were parts of my grandma's life I didn't know anything about. We'd been close when I was little. But as time went by, my family got busier and busier as Witnesses. We moved away. Eventually, there were years between each conversation or visit I had with her.

I was glad now to hear a little bit more about the many good things she'd done in her life. Perhaps that's why she would have asked my dad to speak: as another kind deed. She would let him give the spiel he really wanted to give, in lieu of all the Christmas presents we'd refused.

Have you ever read the book *Ender's Game*? It's one of my top favorite books I've ever read, for reasons I can't describe for fear of spoiling it. Just go read it. I'll wait... That book made me start reading more of Orson Scott Card's work, even though at the time I was a Witness and I knew he was Mormon. The sequel is *Speaker for the Dead*. The title refers to a new role created in the future. A speaker for the dead would come to a place and speak the truth of a person's life—the good, the bad, not judging, just capturing their true being in words.

I wish that were a real construct today. Funerals could be more than an opportunity for survivors to superimpose and espouse their own view of reality. It should be an occasion to see the person one last time—to see their beliefs, their values, their loves and hates, their qualities good and bad. It is when we commemorate the person that lived for the briefest of instants, flaring like a match against the infinite blackness of the cosmos before winking out of existence again.

Life

When I was about sixteen, I went to a get-together. (JWs don't call gatherings "parties." A party is too worldly, where crazy stuff goes down.) As I stood to the side and watched people mingle, I began to get a weird sensation.

It felt like one of those movie scenes when the main character stands still on the sidewalk, and the world flows past him speeded up. Just then Sarah, a girl from the congregation, came up. "Don't you feel like you could just disappear, and nobody would notice?" she asked. I was so surprised to hear she was feeling the same thing as me. We could slip out the door and the get-together would continue on its merry way. Our presence or absence neither added nor subtracted anything to the event.

"You are real.
  You do exist.

While that may sound strange to say,
it is not at all obvious after

you were taught to diminish yourself.
Religious training in self-annihilation
can leave you feeling

invisible,

without
substance."

- Leaving the Fold p. 513

It wasn't until I read *Leaving the Fold* that this experience made much sense. Fundamentalist Christian groups teach you to subsume the individual in the service of God. One must "strip off the old personality" and put on "the new personality" of Colossians 3:9–10. And in the process, you strip away yourself, the very stuff that makes you *you*. I imagine it's much the same process when the Marines get a batch of new recruits.

After making the transition from Witness to post-Witness, I started to catch up on pop culture I'd missed out on because it had had magic. I began reading the *Harry Potter* books. Immediately, I identified with Harry. He was a kid who, for reasons he didn't understand until Hagrid came along, didn't fit in with his surroundings. He had no birthday parties? That was me!

But then I got to Luna Lovegood. Here I truly found a kindred spirit, as *Anne of Green Gables* would say (to thoroughly muddle my literary references). Harry had his close friends Ron and Hermione, and that was something I was missing. Luna knew a lot of esoteric things. Yet she had no friends. Even other members of a society outside normal society viewed her as weird. Now that was really me.

Like a lot of JWs, I'd chuckle when Jeopardy had a Bible category. I'd watch in disdain as the contestants struggled to remember basic facts I'd learned at seven years old. (Of course, I'd be a goner in most other categories.) The one boost to my self-esteem was that I knew more random Bible trivia than ninety percent of people walking around. The Bible was like my own personal Quibbler.

But when I look back, what I really felt like as a JW kid was one of the Hogwarts ghosts. I was Nearly Headless Nick, drifting in and out of rooms, but leaving no imprint on the world. Once I started homeschooling in seventh grade, the actual schoolwork could be done in a few hours. The rest of the day I'd spend lying on my bed, looking out the window. I just watched the world go by.

I loved observing workers. I'd watch the garbage man, the way he periodically worked the levers to compact the trash bags in the truck. How a lineman would work on the wires, and then hoist his collapsed ladder onto his shoulder with a practiced air, to place it on the roof of the van. How an arborist would remove a tree from the top down, slicing off manageable sections of the trunk until it was gone.

Like Nick, it was as if I was eating vicariously by watching others at a meal. I wasn't dead, but I wasn't really alive. I was "no part of the world," just as Jesus had instructed at John 17:16. It was a Christian success story, I guess.

"In my field of paper flowers

And candy clouds of lullaby

I lie inside myself for hours

And watch my purple sky fly over me"

- "Imaginary"
Evanescence

The fun part is you never reach a point where you feel like you're good enough. As you might imagine (or you may just want to kick me for putting the image in your head), a teenage boy that has never thought about sex or masturbated is a mythological creature. It has never existed in all of human history. So right away there was plenty of room for me to be more spiritual. But even if somehow I'd overcome that and become incredibly holy, JWs add another layer to things with their preaching activity.

No matter how active you are, how many hours you spend, you can add more. An ordinary JW can work to become ("reach out," in JW lingo) a pioneer. A pioneer can reach out to serve in a foreign country where the need for JWs is greater. A "need-greater" can reach out to become a missionary. A missionary is the top dog, putting in 130 hours each month preaching. But even a missionary could always add another Bible student, another video shown.

Whatever you do is never quite enough. And since JWs are required to turn in a report each month detailing how many hours they spent preaching, you can grade how godly you are. Even if you personally don't want to analyze your numbers, the elder who collects your report will.

"'A slow sort of country!' said the Queen. 'Now, *here* you see, it takes all the running you can do to keep in the same place.'"

- Through the Looking-Glass

For JW kids, it is super stressful. They live in a world where they are essentially being graded 24/7. All the usual school assignments are graded. But once they walk out of school, they have public speaking assignments at the meetings which get graded. They must turn in their end-of-the-month preaching report. They will be taken aside and receive a verbal warning if the numbers fall below the expected benchmarks.

Informally, a child is being watched and judged regarding hairstyle (for boys, is it too long; for girls, is it too short); clothing (is she wearing a slip, is a bra strap visible, what is the skirt length); kids she hangs out with; movies she watches; how many times she comments during meetings; and so on. Her mother and father are each being judged or graded on all of this themselves as individuals, but also on how well they are doing raising her. How closely does her conduct fit the JW ideal? Parents are super paranoid that nothing be out of place. And in turn, that pressure feeds back to the child in her desire to make her parents happy. No wonder I had IBS.

If a kid has a non-JW teacher or other adult in her life who is unconditionally accepting and supportive, it's such a breath of fresh air. I distinctly remember Mr. Terry, my fourth-grade teacher. I'm sure he was just being a normal nice guy. But his nonjudgmental kindness was so memorable to me as a kid. That was over thirty years ago, and it's still burned into my memory banks.

"The female skull is lighter and its cranial capacity is about **10 percent smaller** than that of the male...

Implicit in these findings is that **man is advantaged** by a greater brain size.

That it is in the **best interests** of *both* sexes for man to take the lead

is also supported by **psychological** evidence."

— *Awake* 08/22/67, p. 27

I could be wrong, but I think it's harder for girls than boys in the organization, and for women than men. Boys are groomed to take the lead. Adult women, on the other hand, really have no role in the congregation beyond what they can do as six-year-olds: preach door to door. Consequently, their value and progress is measured, not in terms of goals reached, but in external things—dress, grooming, and demeanor.

"The feminine woman has learned the art of *pleasing*.

Many were really little tomboys at one time, but somewhere along the way they stopped poking fun at boys and beating them at sports.

Suddenly they became little ladies, eager to *please* instead of taunt. They became feminine in the process.

Unfortunately, some women have not learned this important lesson."

- *Awake* 01/22/68 p. 15

When I decided to go to nursing school, I got a job as a nursing assistant. It was at a company which staffed group homes for adults with developmental disabilities. On my first visit to the main offices, I noticed one thing right off the bat. The place seemed to be almost entirely run by women, bottom to top. And when you'd look at the photos in their cubicles, there were often no men. It was all pictures of their kids. They were single parents.

In my head, I imagined the low point in their life—leaving their bum of a husband, kids in tow, just a high school education at best. But they chose not to remain on food stamps and welfare forever, unlike many other residents in the city. (Latino JWs told us Jamestown, New York had a reputation in Puerto Rico. It was known as a place you could move to and milk the welfare system indefinitely.) Those women went out and got a hard, physical, entry-level job. Lemme tell you, changing adult diapers loses its charm real fast. But they stuck with it. They kept getting promoted until they were running the organization that hired them. I thought it would make a great newspaper article.

I admired capable women in this way, inside and outside my religion. Sometimes I would look around the Kingdom Hall auditorium during a meeting and pick out women I figured would make great elders. I thought they could more than hold their own with any of the men currently in that role. (When JWs gossip, more assertive women in the congregation can get the passive-aggressive label of "elderettes.") It wasn't until years after leaving the Witnesses that I realized just how limiting the religion is for women. What can I say, the male brain at work. But once seen, like those *Magic Eye* pictures, it can't be unseen.

What flicked the switch was reading therapist Bonnie Zieman's excellent books on the process of leaving the JW religion. She writes how incredibly bored she had been as a special pioneer Witness woman (at the time, that meant 120 hours per month preaching). I'd literally never thought of that. My sister hadn't seemed bored. She was constantly traveling to visit friends. Single women could move to another country to preach if they wanted. In fact, there used to be a song in our songbook inspired by Psalm 68:11, all about the large army of women preaching. (Naughty kids would change it to "the army of large women.") It's safe to say the majority of hours spent preaching each year are put in by women, since the husbands generally work full-time.

But beyond the preaching work, there are really no doors of advancement open to JW women. As in most fundamentalist religions, it is overwhelmingly patriarchal. No woman can be a ministerial servant or elder. If a woman has a talk during the meeting, she would never directly address the audience. She is allowed to speak only to the moderator (in an interview), or an assistant (role-playing how to preach). In 2017, a revised songbook was released. It changed one song title from "Guard Your Heart" to "We Guard Our Hearts." There was fear that someone would interpret the former as a woman telling a man what to do—in song.

"A married woman who favors having her **ears** pierced should *rightly* consult her **husbandly head** *first.*"

- *Watchtower* 05/15/74 p. 319

Except in the rare situation that there literally are not enough baptized men and boys to fill the assignments, JW women in a congregation are barred from any responsibility. They can't run the sound system, manage the literature supply, do the accounting, or organize the preaching territory. Well, I shouldn't say barred from everything. They are encouraged to help clean the hall. Handling a microphone on a boom? Not allowed. But pop a mop head on that stick? Perfect.

"Treat Him Respectfully:

The intended victim should remember that
the rapist
is a human.

No doubt there are
circumstances in his life
that have precipitated his behavior.

So although
a woman should not
cower in fear
and permit a rapist to intimidate her,

at the same time she should
treat him understandingly,
as a fellow human."

— *Awake* 02/22/84, p. 25

However, the moment a *boy* is baptized, he is automatically deemed worthy of starting to take on responsibility. This creates odd situations. In my own case, I was baptized at twelve. It meant stepping up to lead from that moment on. For example, maybe I showed up to a meeting for preaching in the morning, and there were no adult men present (not uncommon during the work week). By rights I was expected to conduct the meeting, organize car groups, and generally oversee everything. That possibility terrified me, by the way. There might be women there who had been preaching for decades. But unfortunately lacking a penis, they clearly would be unable to figure out what to do, in contrast to the preteen boy.

In certain situations, a woman may *have* to take the lead. As JWs encourage kids to be baptized younger and younger, to get them locked down into the organization, you can have nine-year-old baptized boys present who are simply too young to run a meeting. Or it may be all women at a meeting for field service. Or a woman may bring a JW man on a Bible study, but take the lead herself, since it's her student.

"But every woman

   who prays or prophesies

      with her head uncovered

shames her head,
for it is one and the same
as if she were a woman

   with a shaved head."

      - 1 Corinthians 11:5

Leaving aside whether it's actually so terrible for women to have very short hair (I knew African American JW women who would beg to differ), women in these types of situations are required to wear a head covering. It's an acknowledgement that men are the head of women. The trouble is, unlike the early JW years, most women don't wear hats anymore (unless it's Kentucky Derby weekend). The result is ludicrous stories every Witness woman can tell of using whatever is lying around. They may end up balancing a napkin, a paper plate, or perhaps a diaper on their head while saying a prayer or conducting a meeting. Clearly, following this rule helps them maintain their Christian decorum.

Most congregations have more women than men. It can be difficult for a woman to find a Witness man to marry. The organization has produced many articles, and even video dramatizations, about patiently waiting on Jehovah to resolve the situation. The upshot is, if he doesn't give you a husband pre-Armageddon, you'll get one afterward, when billions of men are resurrected. You could even score a famous Bible person, like...well actually, I'm struggling to think of a famous unmarried Bible character. Maybe John the Baptist? I guess since JWs teach (depending on the year) that marriages end at death, really any Bible person will be fair game. You'd just have to watch out when the guy's former wife is resurrected. Some of those Old Testament women weren't afraid to shank someone.

Despite so many women in the audience, I'm hard pressed to remember ever hearing a talk that focused on women's issues. It's a huge blind spot for the all-male speakers. I'm pretty confident I never heard the term PMS from the stage in all my thirty years as a JW. Using anecdotes and metaphors to spice up your talks is encouraged. But I've never heard one that referenced getting your period, being diagnosed with breast cancer, going through menopause, or being scared to walk out to your car at night. That, despite being pretty common experiences for a large part of the listening audience. Actually, even JW women wouldn't mention those topics during meetings. It would seem unseemly.

There used to be a public speaking course for all Witnesses called the Theocratic Ministry School. At one point, we worked our way through the book *Questions Young People Ask—Answers That Work*. A section of each chapter was used as source material for students to develop a talk. I remember when we got to the section on sex and body changes during puberty. My friend Lauren, a teenage girl, was randomly assigned the topic. I'm not sure why the organization felt it was material which needed to be presented in this setting, but Lauren went up on stage and bravely covered it, speaking to the other girl who was her assistant. Her cheeks were burning and her eyes were glued to her notes. (I always remembered how embarrassed she'd been. When I got an assignment to schedule student talks years later, I made sure to match the students to the material.)

"The
  wise
  and
  loving
  wife
  recognizes that

  her husband
  has a need
  sexually

  and the
  right

  for that need
  to be

  satisfied".

  - *Watchtower* 08/15/81, p. 14

Since a woman's role in the congregation is that of powerlessness, the patriarchal structure can easily slide sideways into domestic abuse.

"Ahab was too easy with Jezebel.

When he told her about the execution of the Baal priests and she threatened to kill Elijah,

he should have kicked her down the back stairs.

It might have saved her life later. As it was, she was killed by being thrown out of a window.

On the stairs, she could have bumped her way down, and might have learned something."

- Golden Age 06/16/37 p. 606

Most commonly it's the husband hurting his wife, although once in a while it goes the other way. I think most congregations I've been in have had at least one woman who is abusive to her husband and children.

It's the type of parent the JW religion can shield from scrutiny for years, maybe forever. One that wields an iron fist and a leather belt, against kids and spouse alike. These parents (whether the mom or the dad) justify their behavior—and let's just call it what it is: child abuse, domestic violence, pick your descriptor of choice—but they'd justify it with any number of Bible verses.

"Whoever holds back his

rod

spoils his son,

but the one who

loves

him disciplines him

diligently."

- Proverbs 13:24

"Bruises

    and wounds

    purge away

    evil,

and beatings

    cleanse

    one's innermost

    being."

- Proverbs 20:30

"Do not hold back
discipline
from a boy.
If you
strike him
with
the rod,
he will not *die.*

With
the rod
you
should
strike him,

In order to
save him
from the Grave."

- Proverbs 23:13, 14

I especially like the last one. It eloquently captures the *1984*-esque doublespeak—to protect your child, you must hurt your child. When I was growing up, the scripture all children knew by heart was Ephesians 6:1–3. Those verses were frequently cited from the stage in Sunday talks. Children were instructed to be obedient to their parents, and honor them, that "you may remain a long time on the earth." The verse appears to be promising that good children will get to live forever in paradise.

However, countless speakers loved to explain how, in ancient Israel, bad children could be hauled before the local judges by their parents. They would be sentenced to death by stoning. So, the speaker would say, that's what it actually means by remaining a long time on the earth. Your parents won't kill you. You'll reach adulthood, won't that be nice? (A child's only comeback was verse four: "[F]athers, do not be irritating your children.")

During Australia's 2015 "Royal Commission Into Institutional Responses to Child Sexual Abuse," Governing Body member Geoffrey Jackson gave the surprising comment, when pressed, that JWs do not endorse physical punishment of children. Perhaps that is his perception at the tip of the pyramid (and also as a man with no kids, like most of the Governing Body and its helpers). But it's very easy to find articles contradicting that statement.

"A spanking may be a lifesaver to a child."

- Making Your Family Life Happy
p. 132

For my sister and I, my mom's weapon of choice was a wooden spoon. It wasn't heavy, but it packed a mean sting when whapped on your arm, leg, or backside. One day it finally broke, worn out by a million spankings. But by golly, if she didn't have a new one up and running in short order. I remember my final spanking. I must have been around fourteen and sassing my mom. Exasperated, she grabbed the wooden spoon and whacked me. I just smiled. The old spoon had lost its power, and I never felt its sting again.

Honestly, I count myself lucky. In 2001, twelve-year-old Laree Slack's father beat her to death with a thick electrical cable. He was a Jehovah's Witness named Larry Slack. The Chicago, Illinois girl was tied to a bed, gagged, and then whipped when she and her siblings couldn't find a misplaced credit card. Larry, who weighed over 350 pounds at the time, decided to follow Bible precedent and administer "forty strokes less one." He repeated multiple rounds of the punishment. He would pass the cable to his wife for her to continue the beating whenever he got winded. After 160 blows, Laree died of internal bleeding.

In 2006, Larry was sentenced to life in prison. His wife, Constance, was sentenced to twenty-five years after agreeing to testify against her husband. It would be interesting to know if Larry and Constance were ever expelled from the congregation for the murder. If the elders on Larry's judicial committee felt he demonstrated sincere repentance for his actions, he may not even have been disfellowshipped. Either way, JWs have a busy prison ministry. It's quite likely Laree's parents are once again active JWs in good standing.

"The Bible in no way endorses

angry whippings

or ***severe*** beatings,

which bruise
and even injure a child."

- *The Secret of Family Happiness* p. 60

One day I was out preaching with a group of young guys, including two young boys who were siblings. We were talking about food. It's a popular topic for Witnesses. The two boys said that in their house, their mom kept the fridge padlocked between meals. But they were always hungry, as boys tend to be. They explained that they would eat dog biscuits to tide themselves over.

I remember the ewww's from everyone about how gross it would be to eat a dog biscuit. The boys laughed a bit. Now I understand it for what it was: child abuse. Their mom was indeed one of those hard women that cowed her entire family, including her husband. I looked the boys up a while back. They're alive and well at least, so that's a relief.

Congregation elders tend to take a hands-off approach to parents disciplining their kids. I remember one summer convention, when my dad told us about something that happened during the lunch hour. He'd been stationed as an attendant outside, where families were eating lunch on the lawn. A father was spanking his daughter with a stick, and a couple walking past the convention center saw it. They were upset and told my dad to go stop the man. My dad, an elder, hemmed and hawed that it was the father's responsibility to discipline his kids, and it wasn't really his place to step in. The passersby finally left in disgust.

"Whether they do it with **the hand, a wooden ruler** or some other type of **appropriate 'rod,'** parents are authorized by God to use spanking in lovingly disciplining their children."

- *Awake* 05/08/79, p. 27

Looking through the most recent articles, the current stance in JW writings is that non-physical punishment is best, but spankings are okay too, if done without emotion and to the arms, legs, or buttocks. To be totally honest, what really jumps out at me are the article titles: "Discipline—Evidence of God's Love" (*Watchtower* 03/18); "Let Jehovah's Discipline Mold You" (*Watchtower* 07/15/13); "Whatever Happened to Discipline?" (*Awake* 04/15); "The Suffering That Can Benefit You" (*Watchtower* 10/15/78); "Now, This May Hurt" (*Watchtower* 03/01/02).

They highlight the fundamental problem: stern discipline of children is just a subset of a culture of discipline and punishment for Witnesses as a whole. Israel was disciplined in the Bible, early Bible Students believed they were disciplined by God, and each layer of the current organization gets discipline from the level above it—kids from parents, congregations from elders, elders from circuit overseers, and so on right up to the Governing Body. I guess theoretically they are disciplined by Jesus Christ, although he seems to be a lenient parent who doesn't say much.

Kids are at the very bottom of this enormous pyramid, with the crushing weight of a dozen layers above them. And each layer consists of people who have had to receive discipline, and in turn would like to discipline those under them. It's akin to the way a cracked whip is moving faster than the speed of sound by the time you get to the tip. Is it any wonder that by the time you get down to the kids, there's a problem with harsh punishment?

I'm not quite sure how to wrap this bit up. I want to give it a funny, happy ending. I just can't seem to find one. I hate that there are kids who have been abused. I wish the organization would come out and say spankings aren't okay anymore. If they did that, Witnesses would obey. For all intents and purposes, JWs do literally anything they are directed to do by headquarters. I wish Watchtower would print an apology for past doctrines that hurt people. I know that is unlikely. To my knowledge, there has never been an apology or retraction published in over one hundred years.

What is so wrong with apologizing? I'm sure I could cite dozens of *Watchtower* articles touting the importance of saying you're sorry. Maybe they're worried it will hurt their brand, their reputation as God's representatives. Maybe they're worried it could open them up to lawsuits. But just because you're worried about fallout from doing the right thing, doesn't make it the wrong thing.

"Sometimes the **right** thing and the **hard** thing are the **same** thing. I **read** that on a **teabag.**"

- Liz Lemon
30 Rock S4E21

I never much cared for the Bible characters who seemed practically perfect in every way. My favorites were the ones that always messed up a lot, like King David and the apostle Peter. When they came clean and admitted their mistakes, it made me like them more.

And as for reputation? Well, there are literally billions of people in China, India, and the Middle East who will live their entire lives and never hear of Jehovah's Witnesses. Even in the United States—the nation with the most Witnesses—the worst JW child abuse scandals are, unfortunately, barely a blip on most Americans' radar.

In the grand scheme of things, it is an insignificant movement whose importance exists solely in the minds of its believers. It's one of any number of religions spawned during and after the Second Great Awakening of the 1800s. At the time, so many preachers were crisscrossing western New York State it became known as the "Burned-over District." (According to a former Bethelite in my congregation, Bethel researchers had found that our city—Jamestown, New York—held the densest ratio of churches to population in the entire country. I can attest that the number of churches in town was matched only by the abundance of bars.)

The Church of Jesus Christ of Latter-day Saints, better known as the Mormons; the Bible Students, who would become Jehovah's Witnesses; the Seventh-day Adventists; and Christian Science—all emerged from this lively period of religious interest. Most of them unfortunately adopted at least one disastrous teaching. The Latter-day Saints picked polygamy. The Bible Students picked a fascination with predicting the date Bible prophecies would be fulfilled. Christian Science picked using prayer instead of medical treatment. Only Seventh-day Adventists, who are theological first cousins to Jehovah's Witnesses, seemed to avoid any major teachings that would come back to bite them. (They were even ahead of their time and advocated a vegetarian diet.)

So which one of them is the true religion? For most of my life, I would have said unequivocally, Jehovah's Witnesses. Now I would say, is it any of them? Is it fair that salvation would depend on living by the tenets of a single, small religion like JWs? Papua New Guinea has about the same population as JWs have members. What if God decided that salvation was solely through Papua New Guineans?

I can just imagine if a JW were to meet up with Jehovah at the ol' pearly gates.

"Yeah, mate, so actually Papua New Guinea had the road to salvation," God says. (In this scenario, it turns out God has an Australian accent.)

"But I thought Jehovah's Witnesses were the true path?!" says the dismayed JW.

"If I had a dollar AUD for every time I heard that! But sorry, it was the Papua New Guineans."

"I've never even met anyone from Papua New Guinea! There aren't any where I live."

"Crikey, they're a tiny group, aren't they? Only 0.1% of the population. But, you know, they've been right there on their island for your entire life. All you had to do was check them out."

"There's two hundred countries! What was I supposed to do, investigate them all one by one?!"

"Entirely up to you, mate. Probably ought have done, though."

"I don't even speak their language, that's not really fair."

"Ah, Tok Pisin, lovely language. Worth learning, that."

"But I was a good person. I helped those in need, I didn't lie or cheat. Doesn't that count for anything?"

"Ah yes, a common question. Fact is, nope, don't care about that one bit. Sorry about that. Papua New Guinea just really has it going on. Like 'Stacy's Mom,' you know that song?"

"Yes," says the JW sadly, "the breakout hit by New York City group Fountains of Wayne. God, why would you have such an obscure way to get salvation? It's almost like you want people to fail. Or just want Papua New Guineans to feel really superior."

God chuckles and winks.

"Shhh," he says, putting a finger to his lips. He turns to someone out of view. "Oy!" he shouts. "Michael the archangel! Toss some more shrimp on the barbie!"

That's basically how it is for the rest of the world compared to Jehovah's Witnesses. In 2019, Bangladesh had a ratio of one Witness to 517,000 people. That would be like Atlanta, Georgia having a single Witness. How could he possibly preach to every single inhabitant? As a JW, I would have responded that Jehovah will read people's hearts at Armageddon. He will meticulously save every single deserving person. And so, a question arises: if that is the case, what actually is the point of doing the preaching work?

A person could reasonably start to wonder, is it just busywork? It seems to be a lot like the Mad Libs and travel Yahtzee my parents bought Susannah and I for long road trips. Stuff to do so we wouldn't notice how much time is passing.

"By engaging in such
  'holy acts'
  and
  'deeds of godly devotion'
  we will keep ourselves

  so busy
  that there will be

  no time left

  to mingle with the world
  or

  to think

about its ways."

- *Watchtower* 02/15/76, p. 116, par. 12

The organization can't have it both ways. Either every person on earth does need to be preached to before Armageddon, or they don't. And Watchtower writers tell us they don't.

"Jesus was prophetically telling us that his disciples would

not complete the circuit of the entire inhabited earth with the preaching

about God's established Kingdom before the glorified King Jesus Christ would arrive as

Jehovah's executional officer at Armageddon."

- *The Greatest Man Who Ever Lived* p. 50

If it doesn't matter whether everyone gets preached to before Armageddon, then why do it at all? That point was raised in the late 1970s, when many JWs started to feel the door-to-door preaching work was unnecessary. The organization even briefly changed the monthly newsletter's title from "Kingdom Ministry" to "Our Kingdom Service." (The word "ministry" is inextricably linked in Witnesses' minds to "the field ministry," i.e., door-to-door preaching.)

This led rather organically to another thought: that being the case, perhaps the organization itself was unnecessary. Surely, the important thing was the relationship between Jesus and his followers, no middleman required.

"It's *funny* how all living organisms are alike.

When the chips are down, when the **pressure** is on, every creature on the face of the earth **is interested in** one thing, and one thing only: *its own survival.*"

— Dr. Hineman
Minority Report

The Watchtower organization reacted violently to this threat to its existence. JWs by the hundred were expelled from the organization for apostasy. Persons from Governing Body members on down to ordinary rank-and-file Witnesses were purged around the world. JWs doubled down on the importance of the preaching work and entered a period of vibrant growth. My family was among that number. In 1983, my parents were baptized together while holding hands (they were reprimanded for that afterward).

Around 1990, the Soviet Union collapsed. There was a tremendous influx of new Witnesses from Eastern European countries which had banned JWs for decades. Conventions needed multiple swimming pools just to get everyone baptized. It was not until about the year 2000 that growth finally began to slow, thanks in large part to the Internet. Skeptical JWs could go online and chat with like-minded people about any doubts they had. An equally vibrant period of growth in the ex-JW community continues to this day.

The organization is indeed like a living organism at this point. Even Governing Body members are more or less along for the ride. If any of them did have ideas of reforming the religion from within, the slightest deviation from the official party line would get them kicked off the Governing Body. Most likely they would be disfellowshipped before they knew what hit them.

"If my **cathedral** of cutting-edge taste

holds no **interest** for your

tragically
Canadian
sensibilities,

then I shall be forced to
grant you a

swift exit

from the premises...

and a fast entrance
into Hell!"

— Gideon Graves
Scott Pilgrim vs. the World

As JWs who come to question the dogma fade out of the religion, the result will probably be a gradually smaller, but more devoted, core of true believers. It will be interesting to see how the organization evolves, as these more conservative—dare I say, hardcore—members become the leadership. They, in turn, will raise a new generation of even less liberal, less well-informed Witnesses. Some redditors who have entered their post-Witness life describe having JW family members who have essentially stopped watching secular news altogether. Instead, they get all of their information from JW Broadcasting, the media arm of Jehovah's Witnesses. There's now enough content that the organization has a 24/7 stream of shows on its website and on streaming devices.

I know many ex-JWs hope the organization will mellow out in an attempt to hold on to members. That would be great, particularly as regards its policies on shunning, reporting child abuse, and blood transfusions. But I suspect things will actually go in the opposite direction, at least in the short term. Most of the men leading the organization have been at Bethel headquarters for many years. They live and work isolated from the world at large. There is little incentive for them to ease up on policies which haven't affected them for decades.

"When we turn the spotlight

on abusers,

we repeatedly find
not only that

> they come nowhere near
> the standard
> > *they set*
>
> for others,

but

> that they operate
> on a completely different
> set of rules,
> > one that shields
> > them
> > from all the
> > ## hardships
>
> their targets
>   are expected
>   to endure."

- "Creating Sickness,
    Recovering From Religion"
    TheraminTrees

Jehovah's Witnesses are a young religion, barely 140 years old. They're all sharp edges and will defend their honor to a rather fanatical degree. Old religions like the Catholic Church went through that sharp-edged phase too. They had their Crusades, and the Inquisition. But the passing of the centuries has worn down their edges. They are pragmatic these days. If public opinion has turned against their handling of child abuse, the pope can apologize. Dioceses will publish names of priests accused of molestation. The church is a survivor, which means going with the flow. It's hard to picture JWs ever getting as big as the Catholic Church. But if they exist for a thousand years, probably their sharp edges will be worn down, too. I know, small comfort for those being hurt right now.

What do you do when someone hurts you, and then refuses to acknowledge they did anything wrong? I think the answer is different for different people. If it was something illegal, some justifiably do everything they can to bring the wrongdoer to justice in the legal system. The child sexual abuse lawsuits brought against the Watchtower corporations are a good example. In my case, nothing illegal was done, but years of my life were lost to the organization. It was like Count Rugen's suction machine in *The Princess Bride*.

"As you know,
  the concept of
        the suction pump
  is centuries old.

Well, really, that's all this is.
Except that instead of sucking water,

       I'm sucking
          life.

              I've just sucked
                one year
              of your life
                     away.

  I might one day
       go as high as
    five,
      but I really don't know
            what that would do to you."

                  - Count Rugen
                  The Princess Bride

The funny thing is, you don't even realize it's happening until after you leave. It's a very comfortable life-sucker in the moment. And when you finally do realize, well, then it comes: the Sound of Ultimate Suffering. A primal groan, from one's very soul.

"Wish I knew then
 What I know
                now

Wouldn't dive in
Wouldn't bow
               down

Gravity hurts
You made it so

                sweet

Till I woke up on
On the
              concrete"

                - "Wide Awake"
                   Katy Perry

Years of regret hit you like a brick to the temple. It's a bit like getting diagnosed with a terminal illness. I thought I was going to live a million years. Suddenly it's down to eighty. And I burned thirty of them on something I now think is a load of baloney barnacles. I become like Inigo Montoya. I want my revenge. I want to walk into the Governing Body's weekly meeting and fix those pasty, balding, overweight guys with a steely glint in my eye. I would explain the reason for my visit.

"*Hallo.*

My
name
is
Phillip
Kuchman.

You
stole
my
life.

Prepare
to
die."

Ah, it would be a great moment. And afterward, I'd probably still be like Inigo.

"It's very *strange*.

I have been in the revenge business so long, now that it's **over**, I don't know what to do with the *rest* of my **life**."

— Inigo Montoya
The Princess Bride

Wesley recommends becoming a pirate captain. And while that is appealing, I think I'm short a parrot or two to be a truly wonderful Dread Pirate Roberts. The standard recommendation from the ex-JW community is to get some therapy. You need to start to unpack, and then learn how to challenge, unhelpful thinking you don't even realize you have from your time as a JW. I think it's a great idea.

"**Often**, when a witness of Jehovah goes to a psychiatrist, the psychiatrist will try to persuade him that his troubles are caused by his *religion*, entirely overlooking the fact that the Christian witnesses of Jehovah are the *best-oriented,* happiest and **most contented** group of people on the face of the earth."

- Awake 03/08/60 p. 27

Working in the hospital, I'd see these people who just had huge strokes. Maybe their whole side is flaccid, they can't talk, can't swallow. It's awful. They'd go off to rehab. Sometimes they would come back months later to visit. They'd be walking, talking, eating, smiling. Half the time, I didn't even recognize them as the same person. It's amazing how plastic the brain is. If there's a roadblock in one spot, it builds workarounds in another. The new pathways get easier by repetition. (Hey, that was one of the counsel points in the Theocratic Ministry School—"Repetition for emphasis.")

It works for injuries from religion, too. You can build new neural pathways with some guidance and lots of repetition. It is foreign at first. You feel like a doofus repeating positive affirmations, or listing three things each morning you're grateful for. But that's okay. As two famous philosophers once said, hakuna matata. It's like a stroke survivor learning to hold a spoon again. The unfamiliar new exercises will pay off. You just have to be willing to try.

And one thing I've learned, whether it's head injuries or recovering from a high-control group like JWs, is that it's not a straight road. It isn't like a plane taking off and smoothly ascending to cruising altitude. Some days you feel like you're doing awesome. Other days, something happens and you feel like you've slid back seventeen steps. That's just how it is. As the meme says, "They don't think it be like it is, but it do."

"Just keep swimming

Just keep swimming"

- Dory
Finding Nemo

Some ex-JWs get into activism. That's awesome. I think a lot of us might not be here if it weren't for the research of those who came before us. But you don't have to be an activist. It's been said that the best revenge is a life well lived. Going on to have a life that is happy, even though you're not a JW? That is going to Blow. Witnesses.' Minds. It will probably be a better rebuttal than all the Bible research in the world proving conclusively that JWs aren't the one true religion (not that there's anything wrong with that).

For a long time, I had a quote from J. K. Rowling's Harvard commencement speech stuck to my fridge. (The whole speech is worth listening to, by the way.)

"It is

          impossible

to live without
failing at something,

unless

you live so
cautiously

that you might as well
not have lived at all-

in which case,

you fail by default."

                    - J. K. Rowling

If it is necessary to fail in order to succeed, then in that sense I consider my time as one of Jehovah's Witnesses to be my failure. I'm disappointed by it, and it is a loss for me. But I got my failure out of the way first. Now, I can get on with living. But…what exactly? Sometimes I feel like I need to make up for lost time. I need to accomplish something sweeping and stupendous. I must discover all the secrets of the universe. Because otherwise, what is the point of it all? What purpose in life can possibly compete with the JW purpose, being Almighty God's personal representative, part of the 0.1%?

Well, when it comes right down to it, the odds are so infinitesimal that any of us exist. That a particular sperm and egg met up. That hundreds of generations of my ancestors reproduced in exactly the right combinations to produce me. It's crazy! My very existence is quite an accomplishment. Maybe it's purpose enough simply to show my thanks by enjoying my time here, before I vanish out of existence again, or whatever comes next.

I do wish I had a bit more time, to be honest. Maybe not a million years, but there is so much to try out. I bought a ukulele, which I keep meaning to learn. I'm going back to school to become an aerospace engineer. I want to know what all the bugs and trees are that I see during a walk. I want to know the physics of black holes. I want to build a house with my own hands. I want to visit the moon. Sometimes I get paralyzed by indecision. There are so many possibilities, and a limited time.

"Hurry, please.

We have so much time and so little to see. **Wait a minute!** Strike that, reverse it. Thank you."

- Willy Wonka
Willy Wonka and the Chocolate Factory

What if I don't pick the right thing? It's like being in the gift shop at Corning Glass all over again. But I've learned that black-and-white, all-or-nothing thinking is a worldview I got from my religion. Things are rarely all good or all bad.

It makes me think of when I moved to Las Vegas for a year. I didn't especially like it. It was a big city that felt kind of fake to me. Sometimes, it seems like a bad decision. But in truth it wasn't really all good or bad. I don't regret it. I learned what size place I prefer to live in. I loved running in the desert by myself. Every store imaginable has an outlet in Vegas. The sunshine was awesome. Even though I didn't want to stay there, I'm glad I tried it out for a while.

So these days I pick a goal, and start working toward it, with little intermediate goals along the way. I don't always know exactly what I'm doing. I don't have all the answers, like I did when I was a Witness. I was serene in my confidence back then. Now I'm always just a bit off-kilter, a bit unsure.

It's like those *Choose Your Own Adventure* books I read as a kid. I just looked, and wow, they actually still make them. That's pretty nifty. You'd read a page, and then pick between two options, and go to that page and continue the story. You were never sure what the *right* choice was. Actually, I don't think there was one. The journey was the fun part. That's kind of how life is now. I can't see too far down the road before it takes a turn and meanders out of sight. I'm curious to see where it goes.

LIFE

"Chances are you did not choose the religion you profess but you inherited it from your parents. Comparatively few persons actually make their own choice of a form of worship. Most stay with the religion in which they were reared, very often being afraid to make a change even if dissatisfied. This is particularly so in communities that are predominantly of one religion. The person who makes a change may become the object of popular hatred and be deprived of the means of earning a livelihood.

But what should a person do when he becomes convinced that the religion he inherited is the wrong form of worship, that its teachings are untrue and that its leaders are blind guides who are leading him into the way of divine disapproval? Would it be wrong for him to go against the wishes of his parents and of the community by changing his religion? Or would it be

wrong

for

him

not

to

change?"

- *Watchtower* 05/15/59, p. 305

"The truth never set me free

So

I did it myself"

- "Careful"
Paramore

Helpful Resources

To help prove to yourself Jehovah's Witnesses are not the one true religion

JWfacts.com

> Probably the first stop anyone with questions should visit, this website is a wealth of research on any JW doctrine. In a dispassionate manner, it uses quotes and citations almost solely drawn from JW literature itself to highlight inconsistencies and holes in doctrine. Created and maintained by Paul Grundy, a former Australia Bethelite who wanted to establish for himself whether Witnesses are the true religion.

Crisis of Conscience, by Raymond Franz

> Franz was a former member of the Governing Body, a missionary, and helped prepare the JW Bible encyclopedia *Aid to Bible Understanding* (now out of print). His book, first published in 1983, describes the inner workings of the Governing Body, and is an inside look at many of the troubles with JW doctrine. He writes in a very mild manner and examines the idea that one can be Jesus' follower without an organized religion. He also wrote a follow-up book, *In Search of Christian Freedom*.

"John Cedars" YouTube channel
> Lloyd Evans examines all sorts of questions concerning JW practices, doctrine, and JW Broadcasting video productions.

Going Clear documentary
> This documentary about Scientology helps examine the problems with the JW organization indirectly by highlighting similarities between the two groups.

The Reluctant Apostate, by Lloyd Evans
> This book interleaves the history of Jehovah's Witnesses and discussion of its teachings with Evans' personal story of growing up a Witness and attending Ministerial Training School, before eventually leaving the organization. Evans is also the creator of the "John Cedars" YouTube channel.

The Gentile Times Reconsidered, by Carl Olof Jonsson
> A detailed examination of the problems with the Bible chronology JWs use to arrive at the year 1914, particularly the weighty archeological evidence that Jerusalem was conquered in 587/586 BCE, and not 607 BCE as JWs assert.

Apocalypse Delayed, by James Penton
> An exhaustively researched and annotated history of Jehovah's Witnesses. Penton is a retired history professor and former JW. He has also authored two other books, one covering the history of JWs in Canada, and another examining the interactions between JWs and Nazi Germany.

Helpful Resources

To figure out how to leave Jehovah's Witnesses

How to Escape Jehovah's Witnesses, by Lloyd Evans
> Evans compiles tips from his own experience and that of others to explain how it's possible to leave while minimizing the fallout.

JW.support
> A website by the JWfacts.com team which provides much practical advice on how to exit the religion strategically. Especially designed for young people still living at home with JW parents.

To receive moral support for the decision to leave

Reddit ex-JW forum, reddit.com/r/exjw/
> The ex-JW subreddit is a very active forum for JWs and former JWs to vent and find support.

Leaving the Witness: Exiting a Religion and Finding a Life, by Amber Scorah
> A memoir of moving to China to preach underground as a JW, waking up, and eventually leaving the religion behind while still overseas.

"ExJW Fifth" YouTube channel
> Many long-form interviews with former JWs sharing their stories of waking up and leaving the religion.

"Kevin McFree" YouTube channel
> A Brit uses painstaking LEGO stop-motion animation to examine the ins and outs of JW life in a funny, incisive manner.

Unfollow: A Memoir of Loving and Leaving the Westboro Baptist Church, by Megan Phelps-Roper
> Phelps' poignant memoir of waking up, and eventually leaving the Westboro Baptist Church.

Fading Out of the JW Cult: A Memoir, by Bonnie Zieman
> Zieman's personal story of growing up as a JW, and eventually leaving to later become a therapist.

To overcome the psychological effects of belonging to, and leaving, a highly controlling group

Leaving the Fold, by Marlene Winell
> A detailed look at the many troubling thinking patterns a fundamentalist Christian religion like JWs creates, and tools to overcome them. Winell is a psychologist who was raised as a fundamentalist. She helped pioneer the field of research into "religious trauma syndrome." There is also a companion workbook. She holds workshops periodically and provides individual therapy in California and remotely.

"JW Forwardcast" podcast
> This podcast by two former JWs, one of whom is now a life coach, deconstructs the ingrained thought patterns a JW

upbringing often leaves you with, and gives concrete steps to overcome them. Episode 8, "The Blueprint for Happiness," is a must-listen.

ThriveBeyondMormonism.com

Support groups and conferences organized by psychologist and ex-Mormon John Dehlin, which provide practical advice for healing and growth after leaving high-demand religions such as the Latter-day Saints and JWs. Dehlin also hosts an extensive library of helpful podcast episodes at MormonStories.org.

Exiting the JW Cult: A Healing Handbook, by Bonnie Zieman

Another good resource for understanding and overcoming thought processes created by the JW religion. Zieman, a former JW and retired therapist, has written several helpful books, including a short book designed for therapists who may be unfamiliar with the effects of cult indoctrination. Zieman's website also has a PDF for individuals to give their therapist which summarizes the high points.

Combating Cult Mind Control, by Steven Hassan

Probably the definitive work on understanding how cults operate, and how to get out of them. Hassan spent several years in the Unification Church, better known as the "Moonies." After his family helped extract him, he became a researcher of how cults program and control their members, and has helped many former cult members regain their lives.

Forgive for Good, by Fred Luskin

> Luskin, a professor at Stanford University, doesn't mean granting absolution to those who have wronged you. Instead, he focuses on the person that was hurt, teaching practical techniques for moving past feelings of bitterness and anger so you can get on with your life. He has conducted many studies honing the techniques with populations that have every right to be bitter, including families with loved ones randomly murdered during the conflicts in Ireland and the Middle East.

References

Baldas, T. (2018, May 18). How shunned Jehovah's Witness mom killed her entire family. *Detroit Free Press*, Retrieved from https://www.freep.com/story /news/2018/05/18/keego-harbor-murder-suicide-lauren-stuart/620709002

Bro Richard. (2017, October 2). *What's in your go-bag?* [Online forum post]. JWTalk. https://jwtalk.net/topic/32965-whats-in-your-go-bag/

Holmes, D. (2012). *The faiths of the postwar presidents: From Truman to Obama*. Athens, GA: University of Georgia Press.

Printed in Great Britain
by Amazon